SAY CHEESE!

D0943557

SAY CHEESE!

RICKI CARROLL + SARAH CARROLL

A KID'S GUIDE TO CHEESE MAKING

WITH RECIPES FOR MOZZARELLA, CREAM CHEESE, FETA + OTHER FAVORITES

Storey Publishing

The mission of Storey Publishing is to serve our customers by
publishing practical information that encourages
personal independence in harmony with the environment.

Edited by Deanna F. Cook and Lisa Hiley
Cover and book design by Jackie Lay and Carolyn Eckert
Art direction by Carolyn Eckert
Text production by Erin Dawson
Food Styling by Joy Howard
Indexed by Samantha Miller

Cover photography by © Kim Lowe Photography, front, back (m.l. & b.r.); © John Polak, back (top row, m.r., b.l. & authors)

Interior photography by © Kim Lowe Photography, i, ii, iii, vi (r.), vii, 31 (inset), 35 (b.l. & b.r.), 36, 37 (t.l.), 40, 42 (ex. inset), 43, 48, 53, 62, 63, 64 (b.), 68, 69, 76, 77, 94, 96 (t.), 97 (b.r.), 104, 105, 107 (t.), 108–111, 112 (l.), 114, 115, 116 (ex. b.l. & b.r.), 117 (ex. b.l. & b.r.), 119–121; © John Polak, vi (l.), viii, 9, 12, 13, 14 (r.), 15 (b.), 16–29, 30 (b.r.), 31 (ex. inset), 32–34, 35 (t.l. & t.r.), 37 (b.r.), 38, 39, 41, 44, 45, 46 (ex. b.l.), 47, 49 (ex. t.r.), 50–52, 54–61, 64 (t.), 65, 66 (ex. t.l.), 67, 70–75, 78–87, 89, 90 (ex. inset), 91 (r.), 92 (t.), 93, 97 (t. & m.), 100; Mars Vilaubi, 30 (t.r. and l.), 37 (t.r.), 42 (inset), 46 (b.l.), 49 (t.r.), 66 (t.l.), 90 (inset), 106, 112 (r.), 113, 116 (b.l. & b.r.), 117 (b.l. & b.r.)

Additional photography by © adrianciurea69/iStock.com, 2 (b.l.); © Alison Thompson/Alamy Stock Photo, 14 (l.); © atiatiati/Getty Images, 97 (b.l.); © AzmanL/iStock.com, 88 (b.); © cynoclub/iStock.com, 5 (t.r.); © Dorling Kindersley/Getty Images, 5 (b.l. & b.r.); © Floortje/iStock.com, 2 (b.c.), 15 (t.), 88 (t.); © GlobalP/iStock.com, 7 (yak); © JackF/iStock.com, 7 (reindeer); © Joan Vicent Cantó Roig, 107 (m.); © kirin_photo/iStock.com, 37 (b.l.); © lenakorzh/iStock.com, 7 (horse); © Margaret Martin, 122; © Mariona Otero/Alamy Stock Photo, 3; © Michael Winokur/Getty Images, 5 (t.l.); © Nednapa/iStock.com, 7 (water buffalo); © Nikola Bilic/Alamy Stock Photo, 98 (Swiss); © Oliver Leedham/Alamy Stock Photo, 98 (blue); © only_fabrizio/iStock.com, 2 (b.r.); © PeopleImages/iStock.com, 4 (b.); © Photokanok/iStock.com, 7 (camel); © Picture Partners/Alamy Stock Photo, 98 (Camembert, Parmesan); © Shawn Linehan, v, 4 (t.), 6; © Tom Stewart/Getty Images, 2 (t.); © twildlife/iStock.com, 7 (moose); © Valentyn Vokov/Alamy Stock Photo, 96 (b.); © vikif/iStock.com, 91 (l.), 92 (b.), 107 (b.); © ZUMA Press Inc/Alamy Stock Photo, 99

Cover and interior illustrations, lettering, and stickers by Jackie Lay, except page 122 by © Taylor Graphics

© 2018 by Ricki Carroll and Sarah Carroll

Be sure to read all instructions thoroughly before using any of the techniques or recipes in this book and follow all safety guidelines.

All rights reserved. No part of this book may be reproduced without written permission from the publisher, except by a reviewer who may quote brief passages or reproduce illustrations in a review with appropriate credits; nor may any part of this book be reproduced, stored in a retrieval system, or transmitted in any form or by any means — electronic, mechanical, photocopying, recording, or other — without written permission from the publisher.

The information in this book is true and complete to the best of our knowledge. All recommendations are made without guarantee on the part of the author or Storey Publishing. The author and publisher disclaim any liability in connection with the use of this information.

Storey books are available for special premium and promotional uses and for customized editions. For further information, please call 800-793-9396.

Storey Publishing
210 MASS MoCA Way
North Adams, MA 01247
storey.com

Printed in China by R.R. Donnelley
10 9 8 7 6 5 4 3 2 1

Library of Congress Cataloging-in-Publication Data

Names: Carroll, Ricki, author. | Carroll, Sarah, 1984- author.
Title: Say cheese! : a kid's guide to cheese making with recipes for mozzarella, cream cheese, feta, and other favorites / by Ricki Carroll & Sarah Carroll.
Description: North Adams, MA : Storey Publishing, 2018. | Includes bibliographical references and index.
Identifiers: LCCN 2017043996 (print) | LCCN 2017034434 (ebook) | ISBN 9781612128238 (paper : alk. paper) | ISBN 9781612128245 (ebook)
Subjects: LCSH: Cheesemaking—Juvenile literature. | Cooking (Cheese)—Juvenile literature.
Classification: LCC SF271 .C367 2018 (ebook) | LCC SF271 (print) | DDC 637/.3—dc23
LC record available at https://lccn.loc.gov/2017043996

dedication

For Jocelyn,
who at 4 is already
our third-generation
cheese maker

Our family has enjoyed helping home cheese makers worldwide to make delicious, nutritious cheeses for over four decades. We dedicate this book to all dairy farmers whose hard work keeps our glorious landscape productive and viable. To all who have come before us, experimenting and creating the phenomenal varieties of cheeses we know today. To those who pass down their knowledge and wisdom so we can keep this ancient art alive. To our cheese-making family around the world who have shared their kitchen adventures.

To the children of the world, who are our future, this is just the beginning for you. Enjoy and grow with this ancient craft, so you may one day teach it to your children. We hope you find your cheese-making adventures "whey" cool!

In peace,
Ricki & Sarah

CONTENTS

chapter one

chapter two

3

more about cheese
(including recipes)

bonus!
Cheese labels
and stickers at the
back of the
book

chapter three

1

we love CHEESE

What would life be like if we didn't have cheese? Next time you bite into a piece of cheese, remember that it was our ancestors who figured out how to create cheese from curds and whey. During long trips in the desert, they carried milk in pouches made from mammals' stomachs. From the combination of heat and the bumpy ride, the milk separated into solids and liquid, and cheese was born! It was almost the perfect food, easier to store and carry than milk and lasting a long time without spoiling, plus it tasted great and was healthy to boot.

Thanks to this lucky discovery and the work of generations of cheese makers, we can enjoy mozzarella on our pizza, Parmesan on our chicken, and Monterey Jack on our quesadillas, along with hundreds of other yummy cheeses!

it all starts with milk

hand milking

It may be hard to believe, but all the world's cheeses start out the same way — as just plain milk. But what makes each cheese unique? Let's go straight to the source. Milk is mostly collected from cows, goats, and sheep.

Each animal's milk tastes a little different, which makes cheeses taste different, too. Milk from water buffalo and sheep has more fat than goat's and cow's milk, so cheeses made with those milks are richer and creamier in taste. Even using milk from different breeds of the same animal, such as Jersey or Holstein cows, will produce different flavors and textures in your cheese.

What an animal eats affects the taste and quality of her milk. For example, if a cow eats some garlic, the cheese made from her milk may have a slight garlicky flavor. (Unfortunately, feeding a cow a candy bar will *not* give you chocolate milk!) Just as

cow's milk cheese

goat's milk cheese

sheep's milk cheese

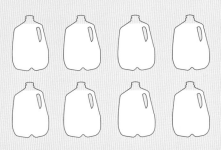

milking machine

For thousands of years, people milked cows and other milk animals by hand, one bucket at a time. This is still done in many parts of the world and for smaller animals. On many modern farms with lots of animals, milking machines are often used.

the foods we eat and the air we breathe affect our health, so too do the foods and air that animals eat and breathe. When the grass and hay are healthy and rich with nutrients, the milk and cheese produced will be richer in flavor and nutrients as well.

When the climate is right for grazing animals, the animals are the healthiest and produce the best milk. If conditions are hard (because of drought or poor soil), the animals do not produce as high a quality of milk. Chemicals and pollution in the soils can also affect the quality of the milk.

DAILY MILK MATH

Most milking animals are milked twice a day. The amount of milk produced depends on the animal's breed, age, diet, and overall health. From 1 gallon of milk, you can make 2 pounds of soft cheese or 1 pound of hard cheese.

Here's how much milk a typical animal gives each day.

Cow: 5 to 8 gallons

Goat: ¾ to 1½ gallons

Sheep: Up to ½ gallon

fun fact

Eating cheese neutralizes the acids that cause cavities and also coats your teeth with a protective film.

But that doesn't mean you can stop brushing!

hi

meet the animals

The beautiful Jersey, with her large brown eyes, gives rich, creamy milk.

Around the world, people make cheese using the milk of a variety of animals. In North America, cow's milk has traditionally been used; in France, goat's milk is very popular; and in Greece, milk commonly comes from sheep. A number of other animals are also milked (see page 7), but backyard farmers mainly use milk from goats and cows to make their cheese.

Cow

Some breeds produce milk with higher butterfat content than others, which affects the amount of cheese you can make. For example, Jerseys produce less milk than Holsteins, but their milk is richer in butterfat. When you use Jersey milk, you get more cheese.

baby, you're amazing!

Babies can do more than sleep, giggle, cry, and poop. Think about it: When a baby drinks milk, it goes down as a liquid, but it comes back up as a solid if the baby spits up. The rennin in their stomachs coagulates the milk, making babies into little cheese makers from the day they are born. Today scientists have made rennet and other acids to coagulate milk to make cheese.

Goats do not eat tin cans, but they do eat poison ivy. An old tale is that if you drink goat's milk after the goats have been eating poison ivy, it can build up your immunity to poison ivy.

Goat

More people around the world drink goat's milk than cow's milk. Goat's milk is closest in makeup to human milk. Its smaller fat globules make it easier to digest (it takes just 30 minutes). Many people who are allergic to cow's milk can drink goat's milk with no discomfort. Goat's milk contains less lactose (milk sugar) than cow's milk.

The milk from Nubian and Alpine goats tends to have a nice sweet taste, even though their yield of milk can be less than that other breeds, such as Saanens.

goat's milk cheese (feta)

Sheep

Sheep's milk is the creamiest of these three, and it's prized for the delicious cheese that can be made from it. Like goat's milk, sheep's milk has smaller fat globules and is easier to digest than cow's milk. In America we use very little sheep's milk to make cheese, though we do raise different breeds of sheep for wool and meat. Sheep are very popular in Greece, where their milk has been used for centuries to make feta. Spain, Portugal, and France also have wonderful sheep's milk cheeses.

sheep's milk cheese (pecorino)

WHAT IS BUTTERFAT?

The volume of fat found in milk is referred to as butterfat. Milk with a higher fat content has more nutritional energy, yields more cheese, and makes a richer-tasting cheese. Butterfat naturally rises to the top of fresh milk as cream. When the cream is skimmed off, the result is low-fat or skim milk. Milk is usually described by how much butterfat it has.

▸ Cream is classified as light, heavy, or whipping cream, based on the amount of butterfat.

▸ Half-and-half is equal parts cream and milk.

▸ Whole milk still has the cream in it. It contains about 3.5 percent butterfat.

▸ Low-fat milk retains a certain amount of butterfat, usually 1 to 2 percent.

▸ Skim or nonfat milk has had all the butterfat removed.

Each milking animal produces a specific amount of butterfat; this amount can vary from breed to breed. Many farmers choose their herds based on the amount of butterfat a breed provides.

0%
skim milk

1%
low fat milk

2%
reduced fat milk

3.5%
whole milk

BUTTERFAT IN MILK

Large, black and white Holsteins produce a lot of milk, but it has less butterfat than milk from some other breeds such as Jerseys.

other animals that produce milk

camel

Camels store water in their humps and give milk to their owners in Saudi Arabia, Somalia, and other sub-Saharan countries.

yak

The shaggy yak provides milk to people in Tibet.

horse

Mare's milk is a traditional part of people's diets in Mongolia.

water buffalo

Water buffalo are milked in countries as different as Italy and India.

The reindeer, or caribou, as it's called in North America, is milked in many Scandinavian countries.

There's even a place in Russia where people make cheese with moose milk!

reindeer

moose

good milk matters

Milk is the most important ingredient in cheese making, so you always want to start with the freshest milk you can find. Buy milk from the closest dairy and from the latest shipment you can. Check for the "sell by" or "use by" date that's farthest from the date you buy it. Ask the grocer which of their milks are local and which came in most recently.

If you live near a farm with milking animals, see if you can buy milk there. If you live in a city, look for local milk in the store or at farmers' markets. You can even use powdered milk for some soft cheeses.

Open the container only when you are ready to start making cheese. Give it a sniff or a taste: If the milk smells sour or tastes bad, toss it. You can't make good cheese from bad milk.

How to Read a Milk Carton

When you are buying milk for cheese, it's important to know exactly what kind you are getting. Here are some terms you may see on a container or hear from a farmer.

▸ Raw milk is fresh milk that has not been heated. It is just filtered and cooled for storage.

▸ Pasteurized milk is heated to a certain temperature to kill possibly harmful bacteria. (See Good Bugs, Bad Bugs below and Buying Milk for Mozzarella on page 86.)

▸ Ultra-pasteurized milk is heat-treated to very high temperatures for longer storage. It is not used to make most cheeses.

▸ Homogenized milk is processed so the butterfat is distributed evenly throughout the milk instead of settling at the top. Homogenized milk makes smoother soft cheeses.

▸ Fortified milk has vitamins or other nutrients added to it.

You may think bacteria are just germs, and the ones that cause disease are certainly harmful. But many, like the bacteria in our stomachs that help digest our food, are helpful. In fact, our lives depend on them!

In cheese making the challenge is to keep the good bacteria happy so they can make our cheese look and taste great. Having lots of good bacteria also helps keep any unwanted bacteria away.

The food industry tries to eliminate bacteria by pasteurizing milk. This heat treatment, developed by French scientist Louis Pasteur in the 1800s, kills all the bacteria. While killing the bad bugs is good for our health, killing the good ones is bad for our cheese! So recipes often call for adding back good bacteria.

the other ingredients

To complete the magic of transforming milk into cheese, you often need special ingredients. You can make a few of the cheeses in this book with just milk and lemon juice or vinegar, while others require specific ingredients from a cheese-making supply company. Follow the storage directions for these ingredients carefully so your "potions" will keep fresh for the longest possible time.

Cultures

Cultures are good bacteria that change lactose (milk sugar) into lactic acid. They help the milk coagulate (set) and ripen, as well as encouraging the whey to drain and working to preserve your cheese. Different cultures also help create specific flavors in cheese. They are always stored in the freezer.

Rennet

Rennet comes from the enzyme rennin, which is found in the stomachs of all mammals and is used to coagulate milk. Today there are ways to make other types of coagulants, even from plants and fungi. Liquid rennet is stored in the refrigerator and tablets are stored in the freezer. **NOTE:** Junket rennet is a very weak form of rennet used to make custards. We do not use it to make cheese.

Acids

Citric and tartaric acids are used to acidify milk in a number of high-heat cheeses. They are naturally derived from certain fruits and vegetables. Before use, they are always dissolved in cool water to dilute them. They are stored in a cool, dark place like a kitchen cabinet.

You can also coagulate milk for some soft cheeses with lemon juice. You might have to use a little more or less in the recipe, depending on the set. Another acid used in cheese making is vinegar. We like to use apple cider vinegar, but any type will work, as long as it has 5 percent acidity.

Salt

Salt draws moisture from the curds, brings out the flavors, and helps preserve your cheese. For most of the recipes in this book, salt is only used to add flavor. A coarse flake salt will dissolve most evenly into the curds. When you buy salt for cheese making, read the ingredients. You don't need iodine or dextrose, so look for brands where "salt" is the only ingredient. Store in a cool, dark place.

Calcium Chloride

Calcium chloride is a salt solution used to restore the balance of calcium in highly processed (both homogenized and pasteurized) milk. It is also often added to goat's milk and store-bought milk to encourage a firmer set in the curds. It is stored in a cool, dark place or in the refrigerator.

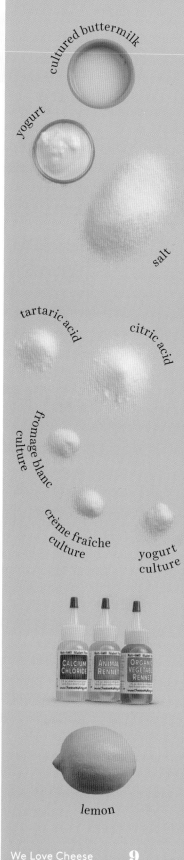

cultured buttermilk

yogurt

salt

tartaric acid

citric acid

fromage blanc culture

crème fraîche culture

yogurt culture

lemon

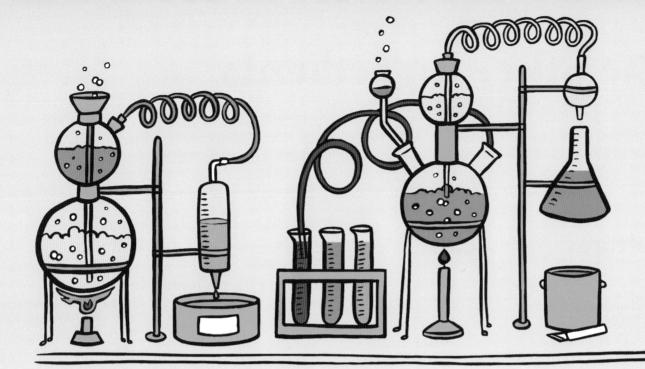

the science of cheese

Making cheese is a simple chemical process. As you mix a variety of liquids together and watch them turn to solids, you become a scientist in your own kitchen. You are transforming milk into cheese with living bacteria for preservation and flavor.

Here's what's happening at each step of making a hard cheese. (Making a soft cheese, like most of the ones in this book, is a little simpler.)

Acidifying

Heating the milk to a specific temperature converts the sugars into lactic acid, which is important for all the steps that follow.

Coagulating

After heating, the fat in the milk is coagulated (thickened) using a bacterial culture, rennet, or an acidic ingredient such as lemon juice, which is stirred into the milk. These ingredients continue the process of creating acid,

contributing to the flavor and preservation of the cheese. Rennet may be used in addition to a culture to thicken the milk and create a solid curd more quickly. Using an acidic ingredient yields smaller curds, such as those in ricotta.

Setting

The milk may be reheated or just left in a warm spot so the bacteria and enzymes can do their thing. Eventually, the milk turns into curds (solids) with clear, yellowish whey (liquid) around the edges.

Cutting

Slicing the coagulated milk into chunks increases the surface area and allows the whey to drain off more efficiently. Some recipes call for stirring or reheating the cut curds to drain off even more whey.

The smaller the curds, the less moisture they hold and the drier the final cheese; the larger the curds, the moister the cheese. Swiss and Parmesan have pea-size curds, cheddar and Gouda have larger ½-inch curds, and Camembert and Brie have very large blocks of curds. Soft, high-moisture cheeses such as fromage blanc can be drained and not cut into curds at all.

Draining

Draining helps remove more whey as the cheese reaches its final texture. Soft cheeses are set in a colander or hung in a cloth bag to drain, while hard cheeses are pressed in molds to remove even more liquid. The longer you drain a cheese, the drier and harder the final product.

Salting and Pressing

Salting draws out more moisture from the cheese and is important for preserving and enhancing the flavor. During the pressing stage the cheese is turned a number of times to ensure even drainage and prevent damp spots from forming.

Aging

Most cheeses are set aside for a period of time to allow their full flavor to develop. Humidity and temperature are important, so the cheese must be stored under the proper conditions to allow the good bacteria to do their work.

tools of the trade

The earliest cheese makers had to do everything themselves, even make their own equipment from whatever materials they had on hand. Some cheese makers still use traditional supplies, such as clay pots with holes for draining curds and woven baskets for molds. These days, using modern equipment made from stainless steel and food-grade plastic is a better option to improve your chances of success at home. If you don't already have the cooking gear described below, you can buy most of it from a regular kitchenware or grocery store.

Measuring Cup and Spoons

A 1-cup measuring cup is all you need for cheese making. The best material for a measuring cup is glass because it lets you see what you are measuring and it is easy to clean and sterilize. For spoons, stainless steel is the easiest material to clean and sterilize.

Colander and Large Bowl

You'll be draining your curds in a colander lined with cheesecloth or butter muslin.

Stainless steel, enamel, and plastic are all fine to use, but, again, avoid reactive metals such as aluminum. The bowl needs to be a bit larger than the colander to allow the whey to collect at the bottom without touching the curds.

Cheese Pot

A 5- to 6-quart pot is large enough to make most of the cheeses in this book. To make feta you'll need one that holds more than 2 gallons. Some recipes can be made in a 3- to 4-quart pot.

Because you will be working with acidic liquids, the pot needs to be made from a material that does not react to acids. Stainless steel, heatproof glass, and enamel (be sure there are no chips in the surface) are all great options for cheese making. A pot with a thick bottom will hold the temperature better than one with a thin bottom.

Labels on image: slotted spoon, colander, pyrex, dairy thermometer, measuring cup, curd knife

Cheesecloth and Butter Muslin

Cheesecloth is a woven cotton material used for draining curds and for lining molds when you are pressing hard cheeses. (**Note:** The material used for actual cheese making is *not* the same as the thin netlike fabric sold in supermarkets, even though it is also called cheesecloth.)

Butter muslin has a tighter weave and is used for draining all soft cheeses and yogurts. You can buy both types from a cheese-making supply store, from various online suppliers, or even at a local fabric store. They can be washed and reused.

Dairy Thermometer

A dairy thermometer is vital when making cheese because it gives a full range of temperatures from 0°F to 220°F (-18°C to 104°C). Candy thermometers don't work because they start at too high a temperature. You can find a dairy thermometer at the grocery store in the gadget aisle. One that clips to the side of the pot is handy, but a digital version is also easy to use.

Slotted Spoon

You'll need a long-handled stainless steel spoon or ladle to stir ingredients into your milk and to ladle the curds out of the pot after they are set.

Curd Knife

A curd knife is a long-bladed knife that can reach to the bottom of your pot. You can use a regular kitchen knife if it's long enough, but specially designed curd knives have rounded tips that are safer to use and won't scratch your pot. A baker's offset spatula that is used to ice cakes also works great.

butter muslin

MOLDS AND PRESSES

Most of the cheeses in this book don't require using a mold or a press, but a couple of them do, and if you become interested in making hard cheeses, you'll need molds. Molds are like the pans you bake a cake in. They give a cheese its shape, while still allowing whey to drain. A press squeezes the curds in the mold, forcing out the moisture and helping the curds consolidate into a finished cheese.

A drip tray is placed under the mold when pressing to help direct the whey away from the cheese. Disks called followers are placed on top of the wrapped curds while they are in a mold. The follower encourages even drainage and helps create a smooth surface.

Making a Simple Press

There are many ways to press cheese, but the easiest way is to wrap the curds securely in butter muslin or cheesecloth and put the bundle in a colander or mold with a saucer holding a weight on top of it. You can also put the bundle between two boards set up on a drip tray or in a sink. Place a jar or jug of water on the top board, and let the cheese drain.

BEFORE YOU BEGIN

Before you begin any actual cooking, here are a few tips to remember.

▸ Always read the entire recipe all the way through to be sure you understand all the steps and know how much time you will need.

▸ Gather all the necessary equipment and ingredients in one place.

▸ Sanitize your equipment and wash your hands thoroughly.

▸ Have a clock or timer handy.

▸ Like bakers, cheese makers have to be very careful when they measure ingredients. If you use too much or too little of something, you may wind up making an entirely different cheese from what you're expecting! When measuring liquids, set the measuring cup on the counter and check the amount at eye level to be sure it's accurate.

Always measure ingredients away from the mixing cup or bowl, not over it, so you don't accidentally spill any extra into the water.

CAREFUL: **Hot Liquid** IN THE HOUSE!
Most of these recipes require the use of a stove to heat the milk. For any of the steps involving stirring or moving hot liquid, ask an adult for help. And be sure to use pot holders!

keep it clean

Cleanliness is a top priority in cheese making. All of your equipment needs to be washed and sterilized before you use it, and cleaned again when you are finished.

When starting a recipe, the best way to sterilize your equipment (measuring utensils, spoons, ladle — everything except the thermometer and the cheesecloth) is to put it all into a pot with a few inches of boiling water, put the lid on, and let it boil for 15 minutes. The trapped steam kills any bacteria that may be contaminating the utensils.

When you open a new package of cheesecloth or butter muslin, rinse the fabric in boiling water before using it. After you've used the cloth, rinse off any cheesy residue with cold water, and then wash the cloth with hot, soapy water to remove the last traces. Sterilize the cloth in boiling water with a little baking soda added, and let it air-dry. After it dries, store it in a closed ziplock bag.

IMPORTANT NOTE: To clean your equipment after making cheese, first wash every item that has come in contact with milk in cold water to remove all cheese residue, and then scrub it in hot, soapy water. The cold water rinse prevents the buildup of milkstone, a film that can be hard to remove before your next cheese-making adventure. If there is some buildup on the bottom and sides of your pot, soak it in cold water for a while before giving it a good scrub with cold water to remove all traces of residue.

THE ICE CUBE TRICK

Many acid-set cheeses require heating the milk to temperatures over 175°F (79°C), which can cause it to scorch and stick to the bottom of the pot. For easy cleanup, here's a trick to use with those cheeses: Before adding your milk to the pot, put an ice cube into it and roll it around until the bottom of the pot feels cold to the touch from the outside. This creates a liquid barrier that prevents a burned mess and helps with cleanup. It also allows you to do less stirring, which is helpful because the stirring motion can break down the proteins in the milk and give you a lower yield on your cheese. Look for the tip box in the recipes that call for this trick.

NOTE: In most of the high-heat recipes you don't need to stir your milk at all until you see a skin forming on the surface. Then just gently stir the top skin back into the milk, avoiding touching the bottom of the pot, which would break the protection barrier.

CRÈME FRAÎCHE

RICOTTA

MOZZARELLA

2

let's make some

CHEESE

FETA

MASCARPONE

CREAM CHEESE

QUARK

QUESO BLANCO

FROMAGE BLANC

It's time to make your very own cheese at home. When you do, you'll be joining the special club of cheese makers who for thousands of years have been creating this amazing food. Not only will you end up with something you can eat and share, but the process of working in the kitchen can be a lot of fun. Who knows, perhaps you will become a famous cheese maker when you grow up!

YOGURT/LABNA

RICOTTA SALATA

PANEER

to make acid-set and cultured cheeses*

1 Heating the Milk

Start by heating the milk to a specific temperature and stirring in ingredients to raise the acidity level. This causes the cheese to set up. The temperature and the ingredients depend on what kind of cheese you are making.

72°
to
86°F

2 Setting the Milk

Some cheeses will set up quite quickly once the coagulating agent is added. Others need some time to develop into curds. The ideal temperature for most cheese at this stage is between 72°F and 86°F (22°C and 30°C). (For some cheeses the temperature needs to be higher, so be sure to follow the recipe directions.) To sustain the proper temperature, wrap the pot in a thick towel or put it in an insulated cooler. Another trick is to set the pot in the sink with hot water (a few degrees warmer than the temperature specified for the recipe) coming about halfway up the sides.

3 Separating the Curds and Whey

As the milk becomes more acidic, it starts to separate into solid white curds and yellowish liquid whey. Some cheeses produce a lot of whey, and others not as much. At this stage, many recipes call for ladling the curds gently out of the whey. (See Way Too Much Whey? on page 22 for ideas about what to do with all that leftover liquid.)

*Acid-set and cultured cheeses do not use rennet to coagulate the milk.

CUT THE CURDS
(but not for all cheeses)

To make some cheeses, the curds are cooled slightly and then cut into smaller pieces to release more whey. In this book, only feta and mozzarella need to be cut. Different cheeses require different-size cuts. The smaller the pieces, the drier the cheese will become.

1. Put the curd knife all the way to the bottom of the pot and cut to make equally spaced lines going in one direction across the entire pot.

2. Turn the pot and cut perpendicularly across the first lines to make a checkerboard pattern.

3. Insert the curd knife into the curds at a 45-degree angle and cut gently back and forth to create layers of cubes the same size as the checkerboard pattern. Rotate the pot 90 degrees and repeat this step one more time.

4 Draining the Curds

The curds are carefully ladled into a colander lined with butter muslin and drained according to the recipe. A shorter draining time results in a softer texture; drain longer for a firmer texture. When lining the colander, use enough butter muslin to cover all the curds. Place the colander inside a bowl large enough to hold the colander with extra space to collect the whey.

While it's draining, keep the cheese away from flies (you may need to cover it) and out of strong sunlight, which will heat it up and may create unwanted bacteria on the surface. If the room is between 68°F and 74°F (20°C and 23°C), you can let your cheese drain on the counter, but if it is warmer than that, place it in the refrigerator. It will take longer to drain, but you will avoid contamination from bacteria and yeast in the air.

HANG IT UP

For soft acid-set cheeses, a fun draining option is to tie the butter muslin into a pouch and hang your cheese in any way that is convenient. Here we're using a banana stand, but you can hang the bundle from a cabinet knob or suspend it on a wooden spoon over a deep bowl.

To make the pouch, tie the corners of the cloth together into a double knot, and use the hole in the center to hang the pouch.

Make sure you have a tray or another container underneath to catch the whey.

5 Pressing and Aging (for some cheeses)

Pressing a cheese after draining removes more whey from the curds. The more pressure you use and the longer you press, the drier your finished cheese will be and the longer it can be stored. This step is used to make hard cheeses and isn't necessary for most of the recipes in this book.

Many cheeses are aged after pressing. This means the cheese is stored at a specific temperature and humidity level to develop its taste, rind, and acidity. Aging is required for hard cheeses and those that need mold to ripen (like blue cheese and Brie). In this book, only feta and ricotta salata are aged.

just drained

whipped

texture

To create a smoother texture in your soft cheese, after it has drained, mix it by hand for a few minutes until it has the texture you like. Using a hand mixer or food processor — set on low for a minute or two — is easier and will make your cheese even lighter and fluffier.

WAY TOO MUCH WHEY?

There are two types of whey: sweet and acidic. Sweet whey comes from making a cheese with a starter culture and rennet, such as feta. Acidic whey comes from a cheese set with an acid, such as queso blanco. Both types contain protein, vitamins, minerals, and some lactose, but acid whey can be pretty sour. Sweet whey tastes better and it would be a shame to waste this useful liquid. Here are few "wheys" you can use it up:

▸ Substitute it for water in bread, pancake, or waffle recipes.

▸ Add it to smoothies for extra protein.

▸ Use it to water tomatoes, blueberries, or other plants that like acidic soil (acidic whey may be too much for them).

▸ Chickens and pigs enjoy it. If you don't have animals of your own, you could offer it to a local farmer.

wrapping and storing cheese

Whether you buy it or make it yourself, it's important to store cheese properly so it lasts a long time and tastes great. Cheese is a living, breathing food, with enzymes and bacteria that require oxygen and moisture to survive. Store all your homemade cheeses in the refrigerator.

▸ Store soft cheeses in glass containers.

▸ Wrap hard cheeses in waxed paper so they can breathe and keep their flavor. If a cheese begins to dry out, place it in an unsealed plastic bag for extra protection.

▸ Today many store-bought hard cheeses are wrapped in a special wrap that allows the cheeses to breathe and helps prevent unwanted mold from forming. If your cheese comes in this special type of paper, keep using it to store the cheese until you've eaten it. If you buy cheese wrapped in plastic, it's a good idea to wrap it in cheese wrap or waxed paper when you get home if you are not going to eat it right away.

yogurt

feta

ricotta

CHEESE recipes

mozzarella

cream cheese

queso blanco

fromage blanc

MASCARPONE

Say mass-kar-POH-nay

Deliciously creamy and sweet, this soft cheese is mainly used in desserts, such as tiramisu (a fancy layered cake), but it can add richness to savory dishes as well. Mascarpone comes from the Lombardy region of northern Italy near Switzerland.

Makes $\frac{1}{2}$ to $\frac{3}{4}$ pound

INGREDIENTS

▸ 1 pint whole milk (not ultra-pasteurized)
▸ 1 pint heavy cream (can be ultra-pasteurized)
▸ Juice from 1 large lemon*

*For a larger yield, substitute ¼ teaspoon tartaric acid mixed into ¼ cup cool, unchlorinated water.

EQUIPMENT

▸ 2-quart pot
▸ Measuring cup
▸ Dairy thermometer
▸ Slotted spoon
▸ Colander
▸ Butter muslin
▸ Bowl for draining
▸ 1-quart glass storage container

Cheese maker's notes: Mascarpone becomes thicker when chilled and more spreadable when brought back to room temperature.

Tip: Using the **ICE CUBE TRICK** on page 15 with this recipe can help with cleanup.

1. After using the ice cube trick on page 15, pour the milk and cream into the pot, and heat over medium heat to 185°F (85°C).

185°

2. If you see a skin forming, stir the top to blend it back in. Don't stir at the bottom of the pot. At 185°F, remove from the heat, and let the pot sit for 5 minutes.

3. Add the lemon juice and stir gently for 15 seconds. You will soon see the curd beginning to form. It will be similar in consistency to a thin oatmeal.

4 Stop stirring and allow the curd to form and cool for 10 to 20 minutes. While the curds cool, line a colander with butter muslin and set it in a large bowl.

5 Use the slotted spoon to transfer the cooled curds into the lined colander. Fold the cloth over the curds and allow to drain at room temperature or in the refrigerator for 1 to 2 hours.

Store in a covered container in the refrigerator for up to 10 days.

IT'S WHEY COOL!

You can have fun with your draining curds by gathering up the corners of the butter muslin and holding the curds up to see the whey draining out. You can see how much whey has collected in the bowl after just a few minutes.

Mm-mm, Mascarpone!

make mini brownie sandwiches!

To use mascarpone to fill cannolis, drain it to a firmer consistency.

perfect for filling dates!

Delicious Dates
Mix a teaspoon of lemon zest into ½ cup mascarpone (this filling tastes best if made a day ahead). Cut 10 to 12 Medjool dates in half and remove the pits. Spoon or pipe (see page 35) a teaspoon or so of the mascarpone mixture onto each date half. Sprinkle a few strands of lemon zest and a pinch of mint on top of each one.

Fun-Filled Strawberries!

Wash a pint of large strawberries and cut off the tops. Use a small spoon to scoop out a little cavity in each berry. Spoon or pipe (see page 35) in a teaspoon or so of mascarpone and top it with sprinkles. For an extra-special treat, dip the bottom of each berry into melted chocolate, or mix a little vanilla or almond extract into the mascarpone.

Blend a teaspoon or two of confectioners' sugar, maple syrup, or honey into a cup of mascarpone for a slightly sweeter version.

Dip a strawberry right into a bowl of mascarpone and munch away — yummy!

CRÈME FRAÎCHE

A sweet, slightly tangy soft cheese, it has a velvety texture similar to that of sour cream. Crème fraîche comes from the Normandy and Brittany regions of France.

Say
krem fresh

makes
1
quart

INGREDIENTS

- 1 quart half-and-half (not ultra-pasteurized)
- 1 packet C33 crème fraîche culture

EQUIPMENT

- 2-quart pot
- Dairy thermometer
- Large spoon
- 1-quart glass storage container

1 Pour the half-and-half into the pot.

2 Slowly heat to 86°F (30°C) over medium heat. No stirring is necessary.

3 Turn off the heat and remove the pot from the stove. Add the culture.

4 Slowly stir for 2 minutes to mix in the culture.

5 Pour the cultured half-and-half into the glass container. Put the lid on and wrap the container in a towel. Let it sit undisturbed for 8 to 12 hours, or until it has the consistency of a thin yogurt.

Store in the refrigerator for up to 10 days.

CRÈME FRAÎCHE VARIATION
cultured mascarpone

Mascarpone is a thick, sweet cheese that makes a yummy filling for desserts (see recipe on page 26). You can turn your finished crème fraîche into a creamy mascarpone by draining it for 2 to 4 hours in a colander lined with butter muslin set over a bowl in the fridge.

An easy way to fill and decorate treats

Chefs use pastry bags for filling cannolis and other goodies and for decorating food. If you don't have a pastry bag, here's an easy way to make one: Put a sandwich bag in a jar and fill it with your creamy delight (mascarpone and whipped cream work particularly well). Cut off one corner of the bag. Make a small snip for decorating and a slightly larger one for filling. Don't squeeze too hard!

cut

Be Creative with Crème Fraîche

delicious on soup!

Pipe funny faces on bowls of creamy soup. (See page 35.)

Mix with mashed potatoes in place of butter.

Toss 1 tablespoon per cup of hot pasta. Divide into serving bowls and top with chopped fresh tomatoes.

mmm, creamy pasta!

perfect parfaits!

Make a parfait with layers of crème fraîche and fresh fruit and a drizzle of maple syrup.

Crème Fraîche   37

FROMAGE BLANC

Say
fro-MAHJ blonc
(it's French for
"white cheese")

makes approximately **1½** pounds

This sweet, tangy treat from northern France and southern Belgium has a smooth, creamy consistency that makes it easy to spread on crackers. Fromage blanc is a great substitute for cream cheese.

INGREDIENTS

▸ 1 gallon whole milk (not ultra-pasteurized)
▸ 1 packet C20 fromage blanc culture

EQUIPMENT

▸ 5- to 6-quart pot with cover
▸ Dairy thermometer
▸ Slotted spoon
▸ Colander

▸ Butter muslin
▸ Rimmed baking sheet or bowl for draining
▸ 1-quart glass storage container

> **Cheese maker's notes:** You can also make this cheese with reconstituted dry milk powder. To use milk powder, reconstitute enough powder for 1 gallon of milk, then follow the recipe.

86°

DIRECTIONS

1 Pour the milk into the pot, and heat over medium heat to 86°F (30°C).

2 When the milk is at 86°F, remove from the heat, add the culture, and gently stir for 2 minutes. Cover the pot, and let it sit undisturbed for 8 to 12 hours at room temperature, or until a thick curd has formed.

6-12 hours later

3 While the curds cool, line the colander with butter muslin, and set it on a rimmed baking sheet or in a large bowl. Use the slotted spoon to transfer the curds into the lined colander. Fold the cloth over the top. Put the colander into the fridge to drain for 4 to 6 hours, depending on the desired consistency.

Store in a covered container in the refrigerator for up to 10 days.

Spread It or Roll It

Whipped fromage blanc makes a delicious spread on any sweet bread, like banana or zucchini.

Make Cheese Balls

Cheese balls are easy to make and have endless variations.

1. Shape the fromage blanc into small balls, about 1 inch in diameter.

2. Roll them in your favorite toppings.

3. Serve with crackers or crisp bread.

SWEET SUGGESTIONS:
chopped walnuts, chocolate chips, coconut, colorful sprinkles

sweet

SAVORY SUGGESTIONS:
herbes de Provence, paprika, dill, curry powder

savory

For a great gift, pack cheese balls in a container wrapped in colorful cellophane with a decorative tie.

perfect for gifts!

Say "kwark" (it means "fresh curd" in German)

FROMAGE BLANC VARIATION
quark

MAKES APPROXIMATELY 1 POUND

INGREDIENTS

▸ 1 gallon skim milk (not ultra-pasteurized)
▸ 1 packet C20 fromage blanc culture
▸ 3 tablespoons heavy cream (optional)

This traditional German cheese is now enjoyed in many parts of the world for its creamy, slightly tangy taste. It makes a great low-fat snack that's high in protein and nutrition.

Follow the steps for making fromage blanc, using 1 gallon of skim milk instead of whole milk. To make your cheese a little richer, mix in the heavy cream after it's finished draining.

Store in a covered container in the refrigerator for up to 10 days.

Make Quark Pops!

berry delicious!

Mix up different fruits with quark to make these yummy pops!

1. Bring 2 cups of quark to room temperature.

2. Lightly purée 2 cups of fresh or frozen blueberries, raspberries, or strawberries with ¼ cup of honey or maple syrup.

3. Add the berry mixture to the quark and stir to combine.

4. Pour the mixture into molds and freeze for ½ hour, then add sticks. Freeze again for 2 to 3 hours, and enjoy!

If you don't have molds, use small paper cups and craft sticks, or try making mini pops in ice cube trays or small plastic snack containers.

YOGURT

Homemade yogurt is rich and creamy with a slight tartness. Enjoy it plain or flavor it however you like. An ancient food enjoyed all around the world in various forms, yogurt was first brought to the United States by Turkish immigrants in the 1700s.

makes
2
quarts

INGREDIENTS

- ½ gallon milk (any type)
- 1 packet yogurt culture or ¼ cup store-bought unsweetened cultured yogurt without any additives

EQUIPMENT

- 3- to 4-quart pot with cover
- Dairy thermometer
- Measuring cup
- Ladle
- 2-quart glass storage container or several smaller ones

Cheese maker's notes: You can use any type of milk, but as always, the higher the fat content, the thicker and creamier the yogurt. Cow's milk makes a much thicker yogurt than goat's milk.
Tip: Using the **ICE CUBE TRICK** on page 15 with this recipe can help with cleanup.

185°

cool to
115°

1 After using the ice cube trick on page 15, pour the milk into the pot, and heat over medium heat to 185°F (85°C). When the milk is at the correct temperature, turn off the heat.

2 Place the pot into a sink filled with cold water to cool the milk quickly down to 115°F (46°C).

3 Sprinkle the yogurt culture (or ¼ cup unsweetened yogurt) into the cooled milk.

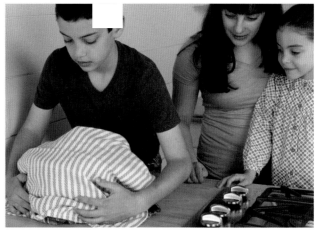

④ Slowly stir for 2 minutes to mix in the culture.

⑤ Cover the pot and let it sit in a warm place (90°F to 100°F/32°C to 38°C) for 6 to 12 hours.

"WHEYS" TO KEEP MILK WARM

▸ Wrap the pot with a large towel and place it in the warmest spot in your kitchen.

▸ Place the pot on a small heating pad set to low.

▸ Pour your cultured milk into smaller containers and place them in a small cooler. If you're using a large cooler, add a few extra jars filled with water at 110°F (43°C) to help keep them warm.

▸ Pour your cultured milk into a very clean slow cooker set to the lowest temperature. Be sure the temperature stays around 100°F (38°C).

6-12 hours later

⑥ Check to see if the yogurt has set after 6 hours. It will become a little thicker when it is put into the fridge. If it needs more time, check it every 30 minutes until it is firm enough to spoon into the storage containers.

Store in the refrigerator in covered containers for up to 2 weeks.

fun fact

In Turkey the word for yogurt is the same as the English word, but other countries use other names, like *kisselo mleko* (Bulgaria), *mazun* (Armenia), *dahi* (India), and *yaourti* (Greece).

Super Yogurt Smoothies

banana

mango

strawberry

Combine different fruits to make your own special smoothie!

- Basic smoothie recipe = 1 cup yogurt + ½ to 1 cup fruit mixed in a blender

- Add juice, milk, or whey if your smoothie is too thick. Use frozen fruit or ice cubes to make a frostier drink.

Experiment with different flavors!

Did you know?
When yogurt first appeared in the United States, some people were excited to learn more, but others made fun of it, not believing that "sour milk" was good for their health.

yogurt cheese and labneh

Yogurt cheese is delicious and easy to make. It's simply yogurt with some of the whey removed. It mixes beautifully with honey, jam, fruit compote, and just about any combination of spices you can think of.

To make it, drain a batch of yogurt in a colander lined with butter muslin over a bowl or pot in the fridge for 6 to 12 hours, or until it looks similar to cream cheese.

it's yummy on crackers!

labneh

To make a Middle Eastern variation called labneh, mix a pinch of salt into the yogurt before draining as above. You can enjoy it plain or flavor it with spices such as mint, dill, garlic, or za'atar. This is a great cheese to drizzle with olive oil, sprinkle with herbs, and serve with warm pita bread.

RICOTTA

Say
ri-KOT-tuh

makes approximately **1½** pounds

Soft, white, and delicious, it is often used in lasagna and stuffed-pasta dishes such as manicotti, but it can also be sweetened for desserts. Ricotta comes from southern Italy, where the name means "recooked." It was traditionally made from the whey left over after cheese making, which was "recooked" to produce a delicious ricotta, explaining the name.

INGREDIENTS

▸ 1 teaspoon citric acid mixed into 1 cup cool, unchlorinated water
▸ 1 gallon whole milk (not ultra-pasteurized)

EQUIPMENT

▸ 5- to 6-quart pot
▸ Measuring spoons and cup
▸ Dairy thermometer
▸ Slotted spoon
▸ Colander
▸ Butter muslin
▸ Bowl for draining
▸ ½-gallon glass storage container

Cheese maker's notes: This recipe uses citric acid to coagulate whole milk, which gives a much higher yield than low-fat or skim. The finished ricotta can be enjoyed right away, or you can salt and age it to make ricotta salata (see page 54).

Tip: Using the **ICE CUBE TRICK** on page 15 with this recipe can help with cleanup.

1 After using the ice cube trick on page 15, pour the citric acid solution and milk into the pot at the same time to mix them. (Or pour the citric acid in first and add the milk second.)

2 Heat the milk over medium heat to 185°F (85°C). Stir the top gently if you see a skin forming. At 185°F watch for small curds as the milk starts separating.

3 Continue heating the milk until it reaches 195°F (90.5°C) or until you see a clear separation of curds and whey. When it's ready, the whey will turn clear with a yellowish hue and lose its milky color. Remove the pot from the heat, and let it rest for 10 minutes.

4 Line a colander with butter muslin and set over a bowl. Use the slotted spoon to transfer the curds gently into the colander. Drain for 10 to 15 minutes at room temperature. For a fresh, light ricotta, drain only until the whey stops dripping. For a thicker ricotta, drain for several hours.

Store in a covered container in the refrigerator for up to 10 days.

Make fun, floaty ricotta-stuffed pepper-salami boats

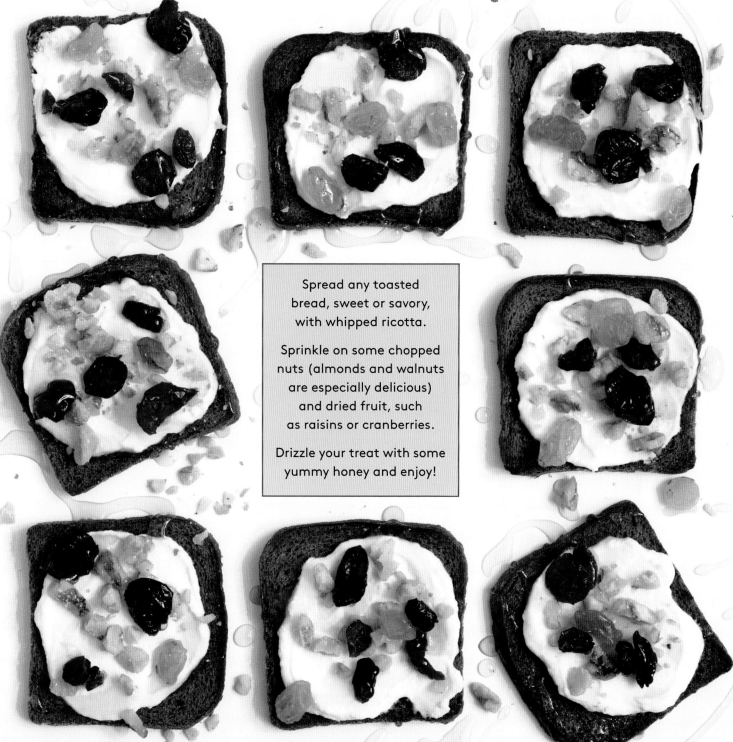

tasty ricotta toasts

Spread any toasted
bread, sweet or savory,
with whipped ricotta.

Sprinkle on some chopped
nuts (almonds and walnuts
are especially delicious)
and dried fruit, such
as raisins or cranberries.

Drizzle your treat with some
yummy honey and enjoy!

RICOTTA VARIATION
ricotta salata

Ricotta salata is a highly salted, pressed version of ricotta that can be aged. After 4 to 6 weeks, the result is a firm table cheese. To make a very dry grating cheese, age it for several months.

1. Let a batch of ricotta drain in a basket cheese mold on a tray or cheese mat at room temperature for 6 to 8 hours.

2. After 6 to 8 hours, carefully turn the cheese out of the mold onto your hand, flip it over, and put it back in the mold. Place a follower and 2-pound weight on top of the cheese. (The lid of a 32-ounce container and a quart jar of water do the trick. For more, see Molds and Presses, page 14). Let the cheese drain until dry and firm, about 18 hours.

3. After it's drained, unmold the cheese onto a plate or shallow bowl. Evenly sprinkle about 1 teaspoon of noniodized salt over the entire surface of the cheese, cover the plate with plastic wrap, and put it in the refrigerator.

4. Salt the cheese once a day for at least 1 week. The salt will pull whey out of the cheese, so pour off the accumulated whey each time you salt your cheese, then cover it again and return it to the refrigerator. As the cheese starts to firm up and lose less whey, you can salt it less often until it is pretty firm, which takes 1 to 3 weeks.

That's a lotta ricotta salata!

QUESO BLANCO

This tasty white cheese from Mexico is traditionally made with cow's milk and usually eaten fresh.

Say
KAY-so BLAHN-koh
(it means
"white cheese"
in Spanish)

makes
approximately
1½
pounds

INGREDIENTS

▸ 1 gallon whole milk (not ultra-pasteurized)
▸ ¼ cup apple cider vinegar

EQUIPMENT

▸ 5- to 6-quart pot
▸ Dairy thermometer
▸ Measuring cup
▸ Slotted spoon
▸ Colander
▸ Butter muslin
▸ Rimmed tray or large bowl for draining
▸ Small plate
▸ Large jar
▸ 1-quart glass storage container

Cheese maker's notes: This cheese holds together like a firm tofu and can be cut into cubes for cooking. Milks with lower fat content create a slightly crumbly but equally delicious version.
Tip: Using the **ICE CUBE TRICK** on page 15 with this recipe can help with cleanup.

190°

1. After using the ice cube trick on page 15, pour the milk into the pot, and heat over medium heat to 190°F (88°C). When the milk is at the correct temperature, add the vinegar and slowly stir to blend it in without touching the bottom of the pot. Usually curds form within a minute — when they do, remove the pot from the heat.

2 Continue stirring gently until you see the clear separation of curds and whey.

If you don't see curds forming, bring the temperature up to 200°F (93°C). If curds are still not forming, add extra vinegar 1 teaspoon at a time, stirring gently after each addition, up to 2 tablespoons.

3 Line a large colander with butter muslin, letting the cloth hang over the sides, and put the colander on a rimmed tray or into a bowl for draining. Transfer the curds into the lined colander.

4 Gather the corners of the muslin and twist them together to form a tight ball. Careful — the curds will be hot!

5 Put a plate and a jar filled with 2 to 3 quarts of water on the bundle of curds and let drain for 2 to 3 hours, or until the curds are nicely consolidated.

Store in a covered container in the refrigerator for up to 10 days. The cheese will become firmer when chilled.

serve up some queso blanco

FRIED QUESO BLANCO

- 1 batch queso blanco
- 2–3 tablespoons high-heat oil, such as safflower
- 1–2 cloves garlic, chopped
- 1 teaspoon tamari or soy sauce
- 1 tablespoon herbes de Provence

1. Cut the queso blanco into 1-inch chunks.

2. Heat the oil in a frying pan over medium heat. Toss in the chunks and stir to coat with the oil. Cook until golden.

3. Add the garlic and tamari to the pan and sprinkle on the herbes de Provence. Stir the cubes to coat with the seasonings. Continue to stir and cook until the cubes are golden brown.

4. Eat right away as a delicious snack or toss them onto a veggie stir-fry.

Experiment with other seasonings. Try cutting the cheese into slices before frying, then eat them topped with salsa!

QUESO BLANCO VARIATION
paneer

Traditionally made from cow's or water buffalo's milk, paneer has a firm, slightly chewy texture, and won't melt when heated. It is made in India, but some say it originally came from Iran and Afghanistan.

INGREDIENTS

▸ 1 gallon whole milk (not ultra-pasteurized)
▸ 1 teaspoon citric acid mixed into 1 cup unchlorinated water heated to 170°F (77°C)

EQUIPMENT

▸ 5- to 6-quart pot
▸ Dairy thermometer
▸ Measuring cup and spoons
▸ Slotted spoon
▸ Colander
▸ Butter muslin
▸ Bowl for draining
▸ Large jar
▸ Small plate
▸ Glass container for storage

DIRECTIONS

1. After using the ice cube trick on page 15, pour the milk into the pot, and slowly heat it over medium heat to 185°F (85°C). Turn off the heat, take the pot off the stove, and let the milk cool to 170°F (77°C).

2. Once the milk has cooled to 170°F, add the citric acid mixture, and gently stir for about 1 minute or until curds begin to form. If you don't see any curds, dilute another 1 teaspoon of citric acid in 1 cup of water heated to 170°F, add it to the milk, and stir for 30 seconds.

3. Let the curds sit undisturbed for 10 to 15 minutes.

4. While the curds sit, line the colander with butter muslin and place it in a bowl. Fill the jar with warm water.

5. Use the slotted spoon to scoop the curds from the pot into the lined colander. Twist the corners of the muslin together to form a tight ball of curd. Careful — the curds will be hot.

6. Place the plate on top of the bundle and set the jar of water on top of the plate. Let it rest for 2 to 3 hours. Once the curds are nicely consolidated, unwrap and enjoy.

Store in a glass storage container in the fridge for up to 10 days.

Cheese maker's notes: Paneer is a great source of protein for a vegetarian diet. It doesn't melt and can be cooked just like tofu in a stir-fry.

Tip: Using the **ICE CUBE TRICK** on page 15 with this recipe can help with cleanup.

peanut sauce

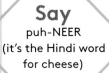

Say
puh-NEER
(it's the Hindi word
for cheese)

To cook, marinate cubes of paneer in your favorite sauce for an hour in the fridge. Pan-fry the cubes for a few minutes in a few teaspoons of hot oil. Serve them up on a skewer with extra marinade for dipping and garnish with herbs and spices.

pesto dipping sauce

CREAM CHEESE

American farm families were making cream cheese in the 1700s. A century later, it was being made in factories in New York. This homemade version is creamier and more delicious than store-bought, plus it's fun to make!

makes approximately

1½

pounds

INGREDIENTS

- ▸ 1 gallon whole milk (not ultra-pasteurized)
- ▸ 1 pint heavy cream (ultra-pasteurized is fine)
- ▸ 1 packet buttermilk culture or ¼ cup cultured buttermilk
- ▸ 8 drops single-strength liquid rennet mixed into ¼ cup cool, unchlorinated water

EQUIPMENT

- ▸ 5- to 6-quart pot with cover
- ▸ Dairy thermometer
- ▸ Measuring spoons and cup
- ▸ Slotted spoon
- ▸ Towel for wrapping pot
- ▸ Colander
- ▸ Butter muslin
- ▸ Rimmed baking sheet or large bowl for draining
- ▸ 2-quart glass storage container

Cheese maker's notes: If you make this cheese before you go to bed, it will have plenty of time to set while you sleep. When you wake up, set it up to drain so you can enjoy a delicious afternoon snack.

1 Pour the milk and heavy cream into the pot, and heat over medium heat to 86°F (30°C).

2 At 86°F, add the buttermilk culture, and stir slowly for 2 minutes.

3 Add the rennet mixture by pouring it through the slotted spoon while moving the spoon over the pot. Stir gently for 1 minute, moving the spoon from the top to the bottom of the pot.

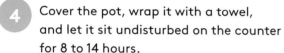

4 Cover the pot, wrap it with a towel, and let it sit undisturbed on the counter for 8 to 14 hours.

5 Put the colander on the baking sheet or in the bowl. Line the colander with butter muslin, letting the cloth hang over the sides.

6 When the curd has developed a few cracks and is pulling away from the sides, gently ladle it into the lined colander. Fold the ends of the cloth over the curds and let them drain in the fridge for 7 to 14 hours, or until they reach the desired consistency.

Store in a covered container in the refrigerator for up to 2 weeks.

66

CREAM CHEESE VARIATION
creole cream cheese

This cheese has a taste and texture between cream cheese and yogurt. It's popular in the South, especially New Orleans, where it's a traditional breakfast food, spread on toast with butter or topped with a drizzle of honey and some fresh fruit.

INGREDIENTS

- 1 gallon skim milk
- ⅓ cup half-and-half
- ¼ teaspoon calcium chloride (if using store-bought milk)
- 1 packet buttermilk culture
- ¼ teaspoon single-strength liquid rennet mixed into ¼ cup cool, unchlorinated water

EQUIPMENT

- 5- to 6-quart pot with cover
- Dairy thermometer
- Measuring spoons and cup
- Slotted spoon
- Towel for wrapping pot
- Ladle
- Colander
- Butter muslin
- Basket mold
- Bowl for draining
- 1-quart glass storage container

DIRECTIONS

1. Pour the milk and half-and-half into the pot and add the calcium chloride.

2. Heat the milk slowly to 80°F (27°C).

3. Turn off the heat and remove the pot from the stove. Add the culture, let it sit for 1 minute, and then stir it in slowly. Cover the pot, wrap it in the towel, and let it sit for 30 minutes.

4. After 30 minutes, add the rennet mixture, stir gently, and let sit for 10 to 15 hours.

5. When the curd has developed a few cracks and is pulling away from the side of the pot, line a colander with butter muslin and set it over a bowl or pot. Gently ladle the curds into the colander. Fold the cloth over the curds and let drain for 1 hour.

6. Transfer the curds into a basket cheese mold and continue draining in the fridge for 5 to 15 hours, until they reach the desired consistency.

Store in a covered container in the refrigerator for up to 2 weeks.

Cream Cheese: It's Not Just for Breakfast!

tic-tac-toe!

Cream Cheese Spreads

Cream cheese combines with many ingredients to make a sweet or savory spread. One tablespoon of flavoring to 1 cup of cream cheese is a good amount to start with. Bring the cream cheese to room temperature before mixing in the other ingredients, then let the spread sit for a few hours or overnight to develop the best flavor. Here are a few suggestions.

Traditionally cream cheese was eaten with a little cream and sugar sprinkled on top.

- Dill and/or chopped chives

- Any flavor of jam or preserves

- Chopped pineapple, shredded coconut, and dried cranberries, topped with sliced almonds

- Mini chocolate chips

- Honey and walnuts

Create pretzel, raisin, and celery butterflies!

Make silly **spiders** with a cracker, an olive half, and sesame sticks and a **panda** with olive ears and a pepper nose!

cute cream cheese creatures!

Turn pistachio nuts into a snake and cherry tomatoes into ants with peppercorn eyes!

FETA

Say
FEH-ta (*fetes* means "slice" in Greek, so this cheese gets its name from the way it is cut to be aged)

Because it is aged in brine (a saltwater solution), feta tastes salty and tangy. The texture can be semisoft to semihard, depending on the milk used, the amount of drainage, and how long it's left in the brine. Now popular in many places, feta comes from Greece, where it is traditionally made with sheep's milk.

makes approximately

2

pounds

INGREDIENTS

▸ 2 gallons whole milk (not ultra-pasteurized)
▸ ¼ teaspoon calcium chloride mixed into ¼ cup cool, unchlorinated water
▸ 1 packet C21 buttermilk culture
▸ ¼ teaspoon single-strength liquid rennet (or ¼ rennet tablet) mixed into ¼ cup cool, unchlorinated water
▸ 2 teaspoons salt
▸ Brine (see page 75)

EQUIPMENT

▸ 9- to 10-quart pot with lid
▸ Measuring cup and spoons
▸ Dairy thermometer
▸ Slotted spoon
▸ Curd knife or butter knife
▸ 2 basket cheese molds
▸ Followers or plates to hold weight
▸ 2 (2-pound) weights (a pint container filled with water will work)
▸ Draining mat or cooling rack and baking dish
▸ 1-gallon glass storage container

93°

1 Pour the milk into the pot. Mix in the calcium chloride solution. Slowly heat the milk to 93°F (34°C) over medium heat. When the milk reaches 93°F, turn off the heat.

2 Add the buttermilk culture and stir slowly for 2 minutes. Cover the pot and let the milk sit for 50 minutes. After 50 minutes, if the temperature has dropped, heat the milk back up to 93°F.

3 Take the pot off the heat, and add the rennet by pouring it through the slotted spoon. Gently mix for 1 minute, moving the spoon from top to bottom. Cover the pot, and let the milk sit undisturbed for 40 minutes.

4 After 40 minutes, uncover the pot and check for a solid curd and "clean break" by sliding the knife 1 inch into the curd at a slight angle. Lift slightly to see if the curd splits, as shown here. If the curd does not split, let it sit for up to 20 minutes longer.

5 Once a solid curd has formed, cut it into ½- to 1-inch cubes by making a checker-board pattern with the knife (see page 19).

6 If the temperature has dropped, heat the curds back up to 93°F and maintain that temperature throughout this step. Using the slotted spoon, very slowly move the curds around for 20 to 30 minutes, to prevent them from matting at the bottom of the pot. The curds are delicate and should be worked with gently so they don't break apart.

7 After 20 to 30 minutes, the curds will have released more whey and become slightly smaller and firmer.

8 Using the slotted spoon, transfer the curds into two cheese molds placed in a baking dish.

9 Place a follower or plate and a 2-pound weight onto each of the filled cheese molds. (A jar with 2 quarts of water works as a weight.)

2 hours later

10 Allow the curds to press for 8 hours at room temperature. During the first 2 hours, unmold each cheese, flip it, and remold at least two and up to four times. As the whey drains, pour it out so it isn't pooling around the cheese.

11 After the curds have consolidated, remove the molds, and cut the cheese into large chunks.

12 Arrange the chunks of feta on a draining mat or cooling rack set in a dish, and sprinkle them evenly on all sides with the salt. Let them drain for 6 to 12 hours at room temperature. Rotate and flip the cheese four times while draining.

13 When the cheese surface feels slightly firmer, place the pieces into a bowl of saturated brine (opposite page) and soak for 4 hours. To brine evenly, rotate any exposed cheese after the first 2 hours.

14 Remove the cheese from the brine, place it on a draining mat or cooling rack in a dish, and cover with a single layer of butter muslin. Air-dry at room temperature for 1 to 3 days. To dry evenly, turn each piece two to four times daily. The cheese is done when the surface feels dry to the touch.

Fresh feta can be stored in a covered container in the fridge for up to 2 weeks without brine. To age it further using brine, see step 15.

15 To age in a brine, place the chunks of feta in a glass storage container. Pour enough storage brine (see sidebar at right) over the cheese to fill the container to the very top. Seal the container with a lid and place it in the fridge for at least 1 week and up to 6 months. The flavor will become stronger the longer it ages. If the flavor becomes too strong for your taste, soak the chunks of feta in a bowl of milk for up to 1 day before enjoying.

TWO KINDS OF BRINE

To make and age feta you need two batches of brine, one for curing and one for storing. Both can be made ahead of time.

Saturated Salt Brine

- ▶ 1 gallon water
- ▶ 2 pounds noniodized salt
- ▶ 1 tablespoon calcium chloride
- ▶ 1 teaspoon white vinegar

Bring the water to a boil in a nonreactive pot. Add the salt, calcium chloride, and vinegar, and mix well. Cool to room temperature and store in a plastic or glass container in the fridge.

Storage Brine (8 percent)

- ▶ 3 quarts water
- ▶ ½ pound noniodized salt

Bring the water to a boil in a nonreactive pot. Add the salt and mix well, until it dissolves. Cool to room temperature and store in a plastic or glass container in the fridge.

the right temperature for feta

If your kitchen is too cold, the curd may have a difficult time setting. Turn up the heat a bit while you are making your cheese — 70°F to 74°F (21°C to 23°C) is an ideal room temperature for cheese making.

If your kitchen is over 80°F (27°C) and very humid, it may be too warm for pressing and drying feta. This would be a good time to make a quick acid-set cheese instead. Try ricotta, queso blanco, or paneer.

Fun with Feta

Watermelon and feta chunks with fresh mint leaves

snack on a stick #2

Cucumber,
pitted kalamata
olives, and
feta chunks

fun fact

According to
Greek myth,
the gods sent
Aristaeus,
the son of
Apollo, to
teach Greeks
how to make
cheese.

MOZZARELLA

Say
mot-za-REL-luh

With its sweet, mild flavor, this soft, sliceable cheese is best eaten as fresh as possible. Known around the world as the primary cheese on pizza, mozzarella can be used in so many other ways! It comes from southern Italy, where it is traditionally made with milk from water buffalo, which is rich in butterfat. In the United States mozzarella is typically made with cow's milk.

makes
1
pound

INGREDIENTS

- ▸ 1½ teaspoons citric acid mixed into 1 cup cool, unchlorinated water
- ▸ 1 gallon fresh whole milk (not ultra-pasteurized)
- ▸ ¼ teaspoon liquid rennet (or ¼ rennet tablet) mixed into ¼ cup cool, unchlorinated water
- ▸ ¼ teaspoon salt (optional)

EQUIPMENT

- ▸ 5- to 6-quart pot with cover
- ▸ 2 measuring cups
- ▸ Measuring spoons
- ▸ Dairy thermometer
- ▸ Large pot
- ▸ Curd knife
- ▸ Slotted spoon
- ▸ Colander
- ▸ 1 large bowl
- ▸ 2 medium bowls
- ▸ Cutting board
- ▸ Rimmed baking sheet
- ▸ Wooden spoon
- ▸ Thick rubber gloves (optional)

Cheese maker's notes: Mozzarella is one of the more advanced cheeses in this book, so it may take some practice to get it right. The success of this cheese relies heavily on the milk you use. Local milk usually provides the best results. See Buying Milk for Mozzarella, page 86, to learn more.

1 Pour the diluted citric acid into the pot, and then quickly pour in the milk so it mixes well. (You can even pour them in at the same time.)

2 Heat the milk slowly to 90°F (32°C). As the temperature approaches 90°F, the milk may begin to curdle slightly.

3 At 90°F, turn off the heat and remove the pot from the burner. Slowly add the diluted rennet to the milk, pouring it through the slotted spoon.

4 Stir gently from top to bottom for approximately 30 seconds. Cover the pot, and leave undisturbed for 5 minutes. While the curd sets, begin to heat 2 gallons of water to 185°F (85°C) in a large pot. This water should be kept hot to be used in step 14.

5 After 5 minutes, take off the lid. The milk should look like custard with a clear separation between the curds and whey. If the curd is too soft or the whey is milky, let it set for a few more minutes.

6 To check that the curds are firm enough, very gently press the back of your hand on the surface of the curd mass. The curds should feel firm against the back of your hand.

If the milk is not forming a solid curd, you may need to increase the temperature to 95°F or even 100°F (35°C to 38°C) over low heat. Once heated, let it sit for up to 10 minutes, checking it after 5 minutes. Be gentle — you don't want to disturb or mix the curd while it is forming.

7 Once a firm curd has formed, cut it into a 1-inch checkerboard pattern (see page 19).

105°

8 Heat the curds to 105°F (41°C) over low heat while slowly and very gently stirring with the slotted spoon. You want the curds to be uniform in size. Cut larger curds into 1-inch pieces, as shown here.

9 At 105°F, turn off the heat and remove the pot from the burner. Continue stirring very gently for 2 to 5 minutes. Stirring too long can make the mozzarella too firm.

10 Carefully ladle the curds into a colander set over a large bowl. Let the curds drain for 2 minutes.

11 Holding the colander over the bowl, gently press and flip the curds in the colander with your hand until they begin to consolidate slightly. This helps remove a lot of the whey. Work quickly, because the curds need to stay warm for the next few steps.

12 Set the cutting board on the rimmed baking tray at a slight angle so that the whey will run into the pan. Flip the consolidated curd out of the colander and onto the cutting board.

13 Slice the curd into four equal parts. This will let more whey drain from the curds.

14 Make two stacks with the quartered curds. Again, this helps drain off more whey. Let the curds drain for 2 to 5 minutes.

   While the curds drain, fill one medium bowl halfway with the hot water from step 4. Fill the other medium bowl with cold water and 1 to 2 cups of ice cubes.

15 Slice one quarter of the curds into very thin strips and place them in the bowl of hot water.

16 Using the wooden spoon or wearing gloves to protect your hands, move the slices around quickly by pressing and folding them in the hot water until they come together and begin to stretch. This should take just a minute or two.

17 When the curds begin to stretch, pull them out of the water and gently stretch them more, either by hand or by letting them hang over the spoon. If the curds break apart like bread dough, they are too cold and should be dipped into the hot water for a few seconds.

18 Once the curd is stretching easily, gently work it with your hands to form a ball. Stretching and working the curds too long will make them tough. To keep this shape, place the ball of mozzarella into the bowl of ice water for 10 to 15 minutes.

Repeat steps 15 to 17 with the rest of the quarters until all of the curd is turned into cheese.

19 Your mozzarella is now finished. You can enjoy it fresh, sprinkled it with a little salt to bring out the flavor.

Store in a glass storage container in the fridge for up to 2 days.

BUYING MILK FOR MOZZARELLA

Mozzarella is fun to make, especially when the curd is being stretched. However, the stretchiness depends a lot on the milk being used. This is the one cheese where temperature really matters, even before you buy the milk. Ultra-pasteurized milk can*not* be used for making this mozzarella.

Only use a fresh, local milk that has been pasteurized at a low temperature, between 145°F and 171°F (63°C and 77°C); the lower the better. Ask your local dairy what their pasteurization temperature is. If you cannot find a source near you, take a look at the Good Milk List at cheesemaking.com for a suggestion. It lists hundreds of dairies around the world to help people find good milk for making mozzarella.

For Help Making Mozzarella

You will find variations of this recipe online at cheesemaking.com and all the help you need if you are having problems getting your cheese to stretch. When this cheese doesn't stretch, the curds when heated look like the curds in ricotta. You can still eat them, but they will taste more acidic because of the extra citric acid in the recipe.

MOZZARELLA VARIATION
making string cheese

To make string cheese, follow the mozzarella recipe through step 17. Then, instead of making it into a ball, pull the curd into a thin rope, allowing the end to drop into a bowl of ice water as you go. When it's cool, cut it into 6-inch lengths and have fun pulling off strings of cheese!

Fun with Mozzarella

fun on a stick

happy or surprised!

Have fun using crackers, olives, peppers, and small mozzarella balls to make silly faces.

Make fancy party food with mozzarella, cantaloupe, honeydew, and basil on skewers.

fun fact

Mozzarella is in the *pasta filata* (meaning "pulled and stretched") cheese family, along with provolone (also from Italy) and asadero cheese (from Mexico).

other easy-peasy (but not cheesy) things you can make with milk

Here are four more wonderful things you can make at home with milk: whipped cream, butter, buttermilk, and sour cream.

whipped cream

Pour a pint of very cold heavy cream into a bowl. Add a couple of teaspoons of powdered sugar and ½ teaspoon of vanilla extract (both are optional). Beat with a hand mixer until soft peaks begin to form. The best part is licking the beaters! Whipped cream will keep in the refrigerator for about 7 days.

Fun with Whipped Cream

Layer chocolate wafer cookies (such as Nabisco's Famous Chocolate Wafers) with your fresh whipped cream, refrigerate overnight, and amaze your friends with this delicious treat!

Celebrate National Whipped Cream Day on January 5!

refrigerator cookie cake!

fun fact

Whipped cream has been around for more than 400 years. In old recipes, it is sometimes called "milk snow" or "snow cream."

butter

1. Warm a pint of heavy cream to room temperature. Pour it into the bowl of a food processor or stand mixer.

2. Beat at high speed until the cream begins to solidify and stick to the sides of the bowl. At first it will look like nothing is happening, but all of a sudden, butter will begin to form! There will be some sweet buttermilk left over.

3. Scrape all the butter onto a clean wooden cutting board placed over a bowl. Using a large spatula, smooth and roll the butter along the surface of the cutting board, scraping it up and repeating the movement for 5 to 10 minutes. This presses more buttermilk out of the butter.

4. Rinse your butter with cold water and continue to work it with the spatula until the water is clear. This may take up to three rinses. Now the butter can be eaten or stored. Transfer the butter into a glass container with a lid. Mix in a pinch of salt (optional).

Keep in the refrigerator for up to 5 days.

buttermilk

INGREDIENTS

- 1 quart whole milk (not ultra-pasteurized)
- 1 packet C21 buttermilk culture or
  2 tablespoons cultured buttermilk

EQUIPMENT

- 2-quart pot with cover
- Dairy thermometer
- Ladle
- 1-quart glass storage container

1. Pour the milk into a pot, and heat over medium heat to 86°F (30°C). When the milk is heated, add the culture, and stir gently to mix in completely.

2. Transfer the milk to a covered glass container, and let it set undisturbed at room temperature for 12 hours.

Keep in the refrigerator for up to 2 weeks.

buttermilk

sour cream

INGREDIENTS

- 1 quart light cream or half-and-half (not ultra-pasteurized)
- 1 packet sour cream culture or 2 tablespoons cultured sour cream

EQUIPMENT

- 2-quart pot
- Dairy thermometer
- Ladle
- 1-quart glass storage container

1. Pour the cream into the pot, and heat over medium heat to 86°F (30°C). When the cream is heated, add the culture, and stir gently to mix in completely.

2. Transfer the cream to a covered glass container, and let it set undisturbed at room temperature for 12 hours.

Keep in the refrigerator for up to 2 weeks.

Fun with Sour Cream

Cut up some vegetables and pile them around a sour cream, herb, and avocado dip!

Peppers, cucumbers, and purple carrots!

sour cream veggie dip

3

more about
CHEESE
(including recipes)

Making cheese is really fun, and eating cheese you've made yourself is awesome! Now you can continue your cheese adventures; there's a whole world of cheese out there to explore. In this chapter, you'll learn about different kinds of cheese, take a walk through cheese history, and find out how to cook up some delicious cheesy fun in the kitchen.

meet the families of cheese

Cheese comes in so many varieties, it's a good thing you don't have to pick just one favorite. Maybe you like a simple cream cheese, spread on a bagel. But you also like Gouda cheese with sliced apples. And who doesn't love some cheddar melted in a grilled cheese sandwich or mozzarella on pizza? Each of these specific cheeses, it turns out, is just one in a family of cheeses. You might say mozzarella is a cousin of provolone, and Camembert and Brie are siblings. If you like one member of the family, you might want to try others.

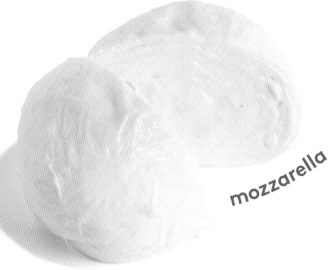

ricotta

Soft Fresh Cheeses

Fresh cheeses are the easiest kind to make at home, and most of the recipes in this book are for this style. These cheeses contain more moisture than hard cheeses and must be eaten soon after being made. They are usually creamy and rich and can be flavored with any number of wonderful ingredients. Many of these cheeses are set with an acidic ingredient such as lemon juice or vinegar rather than rennet.

mozzarella

cream cheese

Camembert

Parmesan

blue

Swiss

Mold-Ripened Cheeses

Mold-ripened cheeses have less moisture than soft cheeses, but more than hard cheeses. They are inoculated with a special powder and aged in moist environments, which gives them unique characteristics. In America, you could say the most common molds are very patriotic, being red (Limburger), white (Camembert), and blue, as in blue cheese. The different molds give these special cheeses distinctive flavors and appearances.

Hard Cheeses

Hard cheeses are usually ripened with a bacterial culture and set with rennet, pressed to remove as much whey as possible, and then aged. The drier the cheese, the longer it will keep, with some lasting many years under proper conditions. Some hard cheeses are aged for at least a year and others up to 5 or 10 years!

fun fact

When 3,800-year-old mummies were uncovered in China, they were found with necklaces of cheese around their necks, perhaps as a snack for the journey into the next world.

ask a cheese monger

Whenever you visit a cheese shop or grocery store with a good cheese department, say hello to the cheese monger. A cheese monger is a person who sells cheese and other dairy products. Cheese mongers are more than happy to talk with you, especially if you use the word "monger"! They usually offer samples and will help you select a new cheese to enjoy or even to create a whole cheese board (see page 104).

Good cheese mongers store cheeses properly so the flavors stay true to their original intent. They know the best season to order certain cheeses and how each is supposed to taste, so they can tell if one has become overripe or needs to ripen longer before being sold.

TIP: If you discover that your cheese smells like ammonia when you open the package, bring it back to the store and tell the cheese monger it has overripened and you need a fresher piece.

QUESTIONS TO ASK A CHEESE MONGER

▸ What is your favorite cheese?

▸ What cheeses are in season now?

▸ What type of milk was this cheese made with?

▸ Who is the cheese maker and where is the cheese made?

▸ What are some words that describe how different cheeses taste?

▸ Did you cut the cheese? (Cheese mongers love this question!)

saying cheese around the world

English: cheese

Czech: sýr

**Danish/Norwegian/
Swedish:** ost

Dutch: kaas

Finnish: juusto

French: fromage

German: Käse

Greek: tupi

Hungarian: sajt

Icelandic: osti

Indonesian: keju

Italian: formaggio

Latvian: siers

Lithuanian: sūris

Polish: ser

Portuguese: queijo

Romanian: brânză

Russian: syr

Slovenian: sir

Spanish: queso

Turkish: peynir

the wide world of cheese

The world is full of wonderful cheeses. Here are just a few of them.

fun fact

The average person in the United States eats about 34 pounds of cheese each year, but that's nothing compared to people in France, who eat more than 57 pounds per person.

U.S.A.

**Colby cheese
Cream cheese
Monterey Jack**

MEXICO

Queso blanco

Edam   Havarti
Gouda   Limburger
Halloumi

NETHERLANDS

U.K.

Cheddar

Quark

GERMANY

Blue
Brie
Camembert
Chèvre
Crème fraîche   Gruyère
Fromage blanc   Swiss

FRANCE   # SWITZERLAND

SPAIN   # ITALY   # GREECE

Manchego   Feta

Mascarpone
Mozzarella
Parmesan
Ricotta

Paneer

INDIA

 fun fact In Italy, wheels of valuable Parmesan serve as collateral for loans to cheese makers. Some three hundred thousand wheels, with a total worth of more than two hundred million dollars, are stored in Italian bank vaults!

GREAT MOMENTS IN CHEESE HISTORY

8000 BCE

Humans domesticate cows, sheep, and goats. No one is quite sure when or how cheese making is discovered, but however it happens, a whole new world of delicious food opens up.

5500 BCE

People in what is today Poland use clay pots with holes to drain their cheese (scientists have found milk residue on ancient strainers).

2000 BCE

Egyptian artists paint scenes in tombs of people making cheese.

1000 BCE

In his famous poem the *Odyssey*, Homer describes the giant one-eyed Cyclops making and storing cheese.

500 BCE

Ancient Greek myths credit the god Aristaeus with learning to make cheese from magical woodland creatures called nymphs, who also taught him beekeeping.

50 BCE

Julius Caesar is emperor and the ancient Romans are making and eating many kinds of cheeses. Parmesan has not been created, though, so Caesar salad is not yet popular.

1000–1300 CE

Medieval cheese makers in Europe are making some of the cheeses we know today. In Britain it's Cheshire, and in Italy, Parmesan. In France the favorite is Brie, which is served at the king's banquets.

1400s

French peasants pay taxes based on how much milk their cows produce, so after the landlord measures, the peasants secretly milk again. The cheese made from that second milking is called Reblochon, from *reblocher*, meaning "to milk again."

1700–1800s

Most cheese in the United States is made on farms as a way to preserve excess milk. The top cheese areas are New York and Ohio. Wisconsin joins them as cheese-loving immigrants from Europe settle there.

1840

Queen Victoria is given a giant wheel of cheddar cheese as a wedding gift. It weighs over 1,000 pounds.

1851

The first assembly-line-style cheese factory in the United States is built by Jesse Williams in Oneida County, New York.

1865

French scientist Louis Pasteur patents his process for heating foods to kill harmful bacteria. The method, known as pasteurization, changes the way most milk, and in turn cheese, is processed.

1666

As London burns in the Great Fire, diarist Samuel Pepys (say "Peeps") buries his treasured wheel of Parmesan. His diary does not say whether it survived, or whether it became one of the first grilled cheeses.

1910

Wisconsin becomes the top cheese-making state, producing 148 million pounds. It still holds that title, with a whopping annual output of more than 3 billion pounds of cheese. (Yes, that's billion with a "b.")

1511

King Henry VIII receives a gift of 100 wheels of Parmesan cheese from the pope (who would have called it Parmigiano-Reggiano). The cheese soon becomes a hit in Britain.

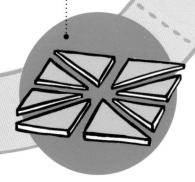

1620

The Pilgrims bring cheese with them on the *Mayflower*. That first winter in New England, they wish they had brought a whole lot more.

2016

More than two thousand varieties of cheeses are made around the world. The global favorite is mozzarella, the cheese that tops pizzas and makes lasagnas gooey.

creating a cheese board

Making a cheese board is a great way to enjoy your favorite cheeses and try some new ones. Arrange them on a special plate or small tray, a cutting board, or a slab of slate or marble. Include a knife for each cheese so the flavors don't get mixed up. Hard cheeses can be cut into cubes and served with toothpicks or mini forks.

Provide thin slices of French bread or a variety of mild-tasting crackers. Dried fruit — apricots, dates, raisins — goes well with many cheeses, or choose a jam or jelly that is nice and thick but not too sugary. Fresh apple and pear slices, grapes, and strawberries also go well together.

For a really fancy offering, try adding these foods to your cheese board.

- cured meats (salami and prosciutto)

- raw vegetables (radishes, celery, and carrot sticks)

- olives (green and black)

- nuts (almonds, pistachios, and walnuts)

Types of Cheese

Three to five cheeses is the perfect amount for one board. You can select similar types of cheese or choose a variety of milk types, flavors, and textures. It's nice to label each cheese so everyone knows what they're eating. If you can, include where each cheese comes from and the name of the dairy.

Fresh cheeses are usually moist, creamy, and mild: fromage blanc, cream cheese, mozzarella

Bloomy-rind cheeses (soft cheeses with a rind you can eat) are usually buttery and rich: Brie, Camembert, triple crème (has extra cream added)

Semisoft cheeses are usually pliable and mellow: Havarti, Monterey Jack, Gouda

Hard cheeses are usually dry and savory: cheddar, Manchego, Parmesan

Blue cheeses are usually soft or crumbly and pungent: Gorgonzola, Roquefort, Stilton

Stilton

Manchego

chèvre

Jarlsberg

Make labels using toothpicks and the stickers in the back of the book, or design your own.

Cutting the Cheese

A cheese ages from the outside in, so it tastes different in different places. Cutting cheeses in a certain way makes each bite taste better because you can taste a little of every part of the cheese. For the best tasting, here are ways to cut different shapes of cheese.

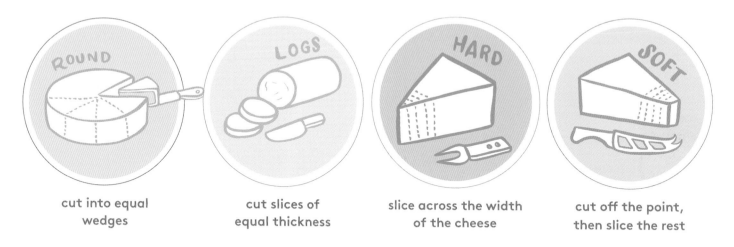

cut into equal wedges

cut slices of equal thickness

slice across the width of the cheese

cut off the point, then slice the rest

Show Off Your Homemade Cheese!

Make a special plate of your own cheeses for friends and family to enjoy. Mix a couple of different ones like creamy fromage blanc and salty feta.

fun to cube

great for dipping

A Cheese Serving Tip

Like many other foods, cheese has less flavor when it's cold than when it is at room temperature. That's because the fat molecules cling together at low temperatures. When the molecules warm up, more flavor is released. So to get the most enjoyment out of your cheese, allow it to come to room temperature before serving.

Hard cheeses need an hour to an hour and a half to warm up, depending on the size of the chunk and the temperature of the room. Fresh, soft cheeses need approximately 30 minutes. A runny cheese such as Camembert or Brie can be taken out of the refrigerator 2 to 3 hours before serving to become deliciously gooey.

Leave cheeses wrapped so they don't dry out, and unwrap them about 30 minutes before serving. (See page 23 for wrapping instructions.)

experiment with flavor

Take a chunk of hard cheese out of the fridge and cut off a bite-size piece. Place the piece on a plate to warm up to room temperature and return the rest of the cheese to the fridge.

Once the piece of cheese is at room temperature, remove the cold cheese from the refrigerator and cut off another bite-size piece. Taste both pieces and notice the difference in flavors. Which one has more flavor? Which do you like better?

fun fact

The rinds of most cheeses are edible, especially the soft ones. You might want to cut off the very hard rind on some aged cheeses, and definitely don't eat any waxed coating.

Add blueberries, sliced strawberries or bananas, or chopped apples for an extra-delicious breakfast.

ricotta pancakes

INGREDIENTS

- 1½ cups flour
- 1 teaspoon baking powder
- 1½ teaspoons salt
- 3 eggs
- 1¾ cups milk
- 6 ounces ricotta cheese
- 1 tablespoon vanilla extract (optional)
- 2 cups blueberries, fresh or frozen
- Unsalted butter, for the pan
- Maple syrup, for topping

DIRECTIONS

1. Mix the flour, baking powder, and salt in one bowl. Mix the eggs, milk, ricotta, and vanilla in another bowl. Add them together and mix until smooth. Stir in the blueberries.

2. Heat a griddle over medium heat, and lightly butter it. Ladle ¼ cup of the batter onto the griddle for each pancake. Try making them into shapes using a cookie cutter on the griddle or drizzling the batter in the shape of letters.

3. Cook until the bottoms are golden brown and the pancakes have a few bubbles bursting on the top.

4. Flip the pancakes, and cook until golden on the bottom. Serve with maple syrup.

super-easy cheesy biscuits

INGREDIENTS

- 2 cups flour
- 5 teaspoons baking powder
- 1 teaspoon salt
- 6 ounces cheddar cheese, shredded
- 2 tablespoons cold unsalted butter, cut in chunks
- ¾–1 cup cold milk, whole or skim

Optional flavorings:

- ¼ teaspoon ground cayenne pepper
- 1 teaspoon chopped pickled hot peppers
- 1–2 teaspoons dried or fresh herbs, such as fresh chives, rosemary, or thyme

Serve hot with butter

DIRECTIONS

1. Preheat the oven to 400°F (200°C). Whisk the flour, baking powder, and salt in a bowl to combine. Mix in the cheese and any extra flavoring.

2. Add the butter and cut it into the flour mixture with your fingers or a pastry blender until it resembles coarse crumbs.

3. Add the milk a little at a time, mixing until you have a soft dough.

4. Place the dough on a lightly floured surface and knead it a few times, sprinkling the ball with a little bit more flour if it's too sticky. Pat the dough into a circle about ½ inch thick. Use a floured cookie cutter to cut out biscuits. Place them on a baking sheet and bake until lightly browned, 12 to 15 minutes.

quick and crispy quesadillas

SERVES 4–8

INGREDIENTS

- ▸ 8 medium corn or flour tortillas
- ▸ 1 pound cheese, shredded (sharp cheddar, Monterey Jack, or a mix)
- ▸ Salsa and sour cream for dipping

Optional fillings:

- ▸ 1 (15-ounce) can black beans, rinsed and drained
- ▸ Finely chopped red onion
- ▸ Diced jalapeño peppers
- ▸ Sliced avocado

Serve the salsa and sour cream in ramekins or small bowls.

DIRECTIONS

1. Heat a cast-iron or other nonstick frying pan over medium heat.

2. Place a tortilla in the pan, add cheese and other fillings, and cover with a second tortilla.

3. Cook on one side until the cheese begins to melt. Flip it over and cook until the cheese is melted and the tortilla is brown in spots.

4. Repeat with the remaining tortillas and fillings.

5. Cut each quesadilla into quarters and serve with salsa and sour cream.

eat quesadillas while hot!

Add as many extra fillings as you like!

great grilled cheese combos

1. Melt 1 tablespoon of butter over medium heat in a cast iron or other nonstick frying pan.

2. Assemble your sandwich using the ingredients suggested here, or create your own gourmet version.

3. Put your sandwich in the pan, and cook the first side for 3 to 5 minutes, or until golden brown.

4. Flip it over, adding a little more butter to the pan if needed. Cook until the other side is also golden brown and the cheese is melted.

▸ **Note:** Or you can butter each slice of bread generously on the outside, layer in the ingredients, and then cook in a frying pan, turning until golden brown on both sides.

mozzarella and pepperoni   **cheddar and apples**

Great for Dessert, Too!

Try a sweet grilled cheese using:

- mascarpone and your favorite jam
- cream cheese with honey and chopped nuts
- ricotta and hazelnut-chocolate spread

ricotta and tomato

mozzarella and pesto

marvelous mac & cheese

INGREDIENTS

- ½ pound pasta (bows, wheels, and mini shells are fun)
- 3 tablespoons butter
- 3 tablespoons flour
- 1 teaspoon dry mustard
- 3½ cups milk
- 1 cup grated cheddar cheese
- ½ cup grated Parmesan or Swiss cheese
- Salt and freshly ground black pepper
- ¾ cup bread crumbs
- ½ teaspoon dried oregano
- ½ teaspoon dried basil
- 1 teaspoon olive oil

DIRECTIONS

1. Preheat the oven to 350°F (180°C). Grease an 8- by 8-inch or 9- by 9-inch baking dish and set aside.

2. Cook the pasta for half the time recommended on the package. Rinse under cold running water and set aside.

3. While the pasta cooks, melt the butter over medium heat in a small pot. Add the flour and mustard and cook, stirring constantly, for 2 to 3 minutes.

4. Stir in the milk very slowly, whisking the whole time to avoid lumps. Cook until thickened, but be careful not to boil the milk.

5. Take the pan off the heat and stir in the cheeses until they melt. Mix in some salt and pepper to taste, then add the pasta and stir until combined. Pour the mixture into the prepared baking dish.

6. Mix the bread crumbs, herbs, and oil in a small bowl. Sprinkle the mixture over the macaroni and cheese, and bake for 20 minutes, or until bubbly and brown.

mini greek pizzas

INGREDIENTS

- 8 English muffins, cut in half
- 1 cup tomato or pizza sauce
- 8 ounces feta cheese, broken up
- 1 green pepper, diced
- 1 small red onion, diced
- ½ cup pitted black olives, sliced in half
- ¼ cup chopped fresh parsley

DIRECTIONS

1. Heat the oven to 375°F (190°C). Put the muffin halves on a baking sheet.

2. Spoon some sauce on each muffin. Top with feta, peppers, onions, and olives.

3. Bake for 10 to 12 minutes, or until heated through.

4. Sprinkle with the parsley before serving.

baked and ready to eat

Turn the page for more pizza ideas!

115

More mini pizza combos to try

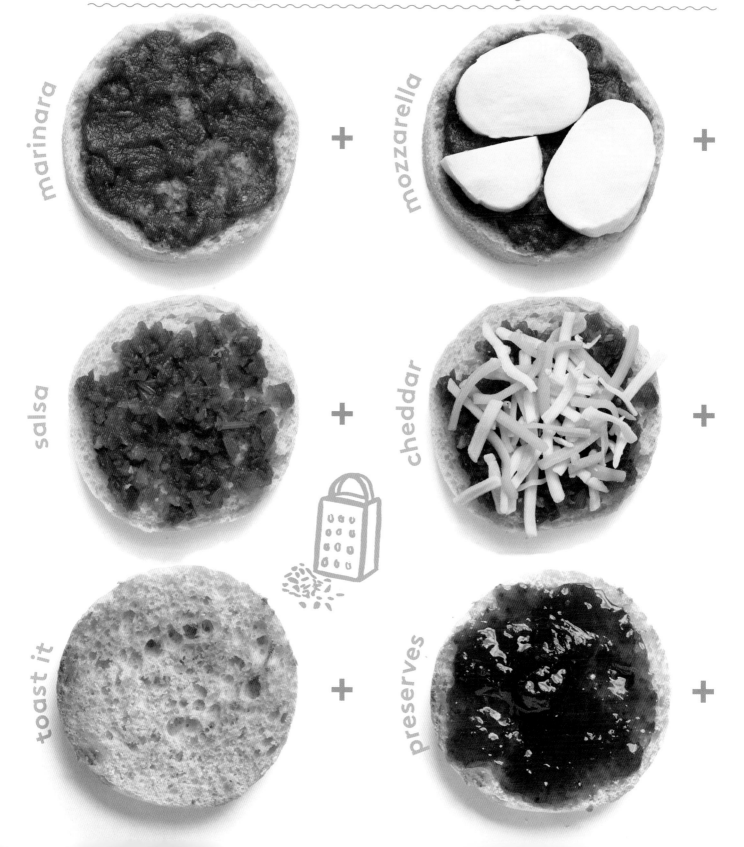

marinara + mozzarella +

salsa + cheddar +

toast it + preserves +

tomato and basil

traditional

Marinara sauce, mozzarella, tomatoes, and basil

=

beans

tex-mex

Salsa, cheddar and/or Monterey Jack cheese, black beans

=

ricotta stripes

breakfast

Strawberry preserves and ricotta

=

family fondue night

INGREDIENTS

- ▸ 2 cups grated Gruyère cheese
- ▸ 1½ cups grated Swiss cheese
- ▸ 2 tablespoons cornstarch
- ▸ 1 cup chicken or vegetable broth
- ▸ 1 tablespoon finely diced garlic
- ▸ Squeeze of fresh lemon juice
- ▸ ¼ teaspoon freshly ground black pepper
- ▸ ¼ teaspoon ground nutmeg
- ▸ Pinch of ground paprika

DIRECTIONS

1. Put the Gruyère and Swiss in a large bowl. Sprinkle the cornstarch on top and mix until evenly coated.

2. Combine the broth, garlic, and lemon juice in a fondue pot or saucepan, and bring it to a simmer over medium heat.

3. Turn the heat to medium low, and add the cheese mixture by small handfuls while stirring constantly with a wooden spoon.

4. When the cheese mixture is completely melted (about the consistency of honey), mix in the spices.

5. Bring the pot to the table and dive in!

Big Dippers:
Chunks of French bread, lightly steamed broccoli florets, apple slices, carrot pieces, baby potatoes, sliced sausage — the possibilities are endless. Everything tastes good dipped in cheese!

itty-bitty lasagnas

MAKES 6–8

INGREDIENTS

- ▸ 1 pound lasagna noodles
- ▸ 1 tablespoon olive oil
- ▸ 1 (32-ounce) jar spaghetti or marinara sauce
- ▸ 2 cups ricotta cheese
- ▸ 1 pound sweet Italian sausage, or ground beef or turkey, cooked and crumbled (or chopped cooked vegetables)
- ▸ 6 cups shredded mozzarella cheese
- ▸ 1 cup grated Parmesan cheese
- ▸ ½ cup chopped fresh basil or pesto

DIRECTIONS

1. Preheat oven to 300°F (150°C).

2. Cook the noodles according to the package directions. Drain and toss with the oil to keep them from sticking together.

3. Spread a spoonful of sauce on the bottom of each pan, then build the lasagnas in thin layers of noodles, ricotta, meat or veggies, sauce, and mozzarella until the pans are nearly full. Finish with another layer of sauce sprinkled with mozzarella. Top with Parmesan.

4. Bake for 10 to 12 minutes, or until the cheese is melted and the sauce is bubbling around the edges. Sprinkle with fresh basil or drizzle with pesto and dig in!

use mini pans

Make your own personal lasagna with your favorite fillings!

Have a party where your guests create their own!

berry good cream cheese pie

INGREDIENTS

- 2¼ cups raspberries, strawberries, or mixed berries, fresh or frozen (thaw first)
- 1½ cups whipped cream (page 88)
- 16 ounces cream cheese, softened, (page 64)
- ¼ cup confectioners' sugar
- 1 graham cracker pie crust (store-bought or homemade)

DIRECTIONS

1. Reserve a few berries for decoration. Place the rest in a blender or food processor and purée until slightly chunky.

2. Mix the whipped cream and the cream cheese in a large bowl. Add the sugar and beat with an electric mixer until smooth.

3. Fold the berry purée into the cream cheese mixture with a spatula until well combined.

4. Pour the filling into the graham cracker crust, smoothing the top with a spatula.

5. Cover with plastic wrap and refrigerate until firm, about 4 hours.

6. Before serving, decorate with squirts of whipped cream and whole or sliced berries.

a free gift for you

We hope you will have as much fun at home creating these yummy cheeses as we all did in our kitchens. To help you get started, visit us at www.cheesemaking.com/saycheese to pick up a free gift and learn more about making cheese. To ask questions and tell us about your own cheese-making adventures, you can reach us at info@cheesemaking.com. Our friendly cheese makers are always happy to talk about cheese!

acknowledgments

We had a really "gouda" time with the all the kids making the cheeses in this book. A big hug and thank "ewe" to Addison, Asha, Aydan, Declan, Eamon, Eilish, Francesca, Gabrielle, Harris, Inez, Ishan, Lulu, Reyna, Sofia, Zadie, and Zoe.

We also want to thank all the great people at Storey who put their love into making this book a reality. A big shout-out to our ever-so-patient and gracious editor, Lisa Hiley, along with the fabulous team behind the dream: Carolyn Eckert, Deanna Cook, Mars Vilaubi, and Erin Dawson. Thanks also to John Polack and Kim Lowe, photographers, as well as Joy Howard and Jon Adolph.

Another special thank you has to go to Jeri Case, who is always right there any time help is needed.

In love and peace,
Ricki & Sarah

metric conversions

Unless you have finely calibrated measuring equipment, conversions between US and metric measurements will be somewhat inexact. It's important to convert the measurements for all of the ingredients in a recipe to maintain the same proportions as the original.

Weight

TO CONVERT	TO	MULTIPLY
ounces	grams	ounces by 28.35
pounds	grams	pounds by 453.5
pounds	kilograms	pounds by 0.45

US	METRIC
0.035 ounce	1 gram
¼ ounce	7 grams
½ ounce	14 grams
1 ounce	28 grams
8 ounces	228 grams
16 ounces (1 pound)	454 grams

Volume

TO CONVERT	TO	MULTIPLY
teaspoons	milliliters	teaspoons by 4.93
tablespoons	milliliters	tablespoons by 14.79
fluid ounces	milliliters	fluid ounces by 29.57
cups	milliliters	cups by 236.59
cups	liters	cups by 0.24
pints	milliliters	pints by 473.18
pints	liters	pints by 0.473
quarts	milliliters	quarts by 946.36
quarts	liters	quarts by 0.946
gallons	liters	gallons by 3.785

US	METRIC
1 teaspoon	5 milliliters
1 tablespoon	15 milliliters
¼ cup	60 milliliters
½ cup	120 milliliters
1 cup	230 milliliters
1¼ cups	300 milliliters
1½ cups	360 milliliters
2 cups	460 milliliters
2½ cups	600 milliliters
3 cups	700 milliliters
4 cups (1 quart)	0.95 liter
4 quarts (1 gallon)	3.8 liters

Temperature

TO CONVERT FAHRENHEIT TO CELSIUS: subtract 32 from Fahrenheit temperature, multiply by 5, then divide by 9.

index

Page numbers in *italic* indicate illustrations and photographs.

Feed Your Mind *and* Your Belly with More Books from Storey

by Deanna F. Cook
Aspiring bakers ages 8–12 can make their favorite treats — from pizza and breads to cookies and cupcakes — with these 50 easy, kid-tested recipes. Lively step-by-step photos teach essential kitchen skills like kneading dough and rolling out a piecrust.

by Deanna F. Cook
This fresh, fun cookbook teaches basic cooking techniques in kid-friendly language, with dozens of recipes (and stickers!) for favorite foods like French toast, homemade granola, buffalo chicken fingers, tortilla chips, and much more.

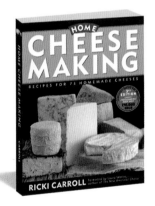

by Ricki Carroll
This best-selling primer to making artisanal-quality soft and hard cheeses includes recipes for sour cream, yogurt, kefir, and buttermilk. In-depth chapters on ingredients, equipment, and techniques teach you everything you need to know before trying out the 75 classic recipes.

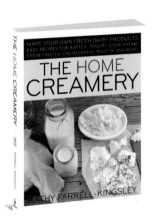

by Kathy Farrell-Kingsley
Make your own dairy products with these easy methods for butter, yogurt, sour cream, and more. Step-by-step instructions are augmented by 75 delicious recipes that use your freshly made dairy, from Apple Coffee Cake with Caramel Glaze to Zucchini Triangles.

Join the conversation. Share your experience with this book, learn more about Storey Publishing's authors, and read original essays and book excerpts at storey.com.

Look for our books wherever quality books are sold or call 800-441-5700.

cheese board flags

Fold each sticker over a toothpick and fill in the name to mark each cheese on your cheese plate.

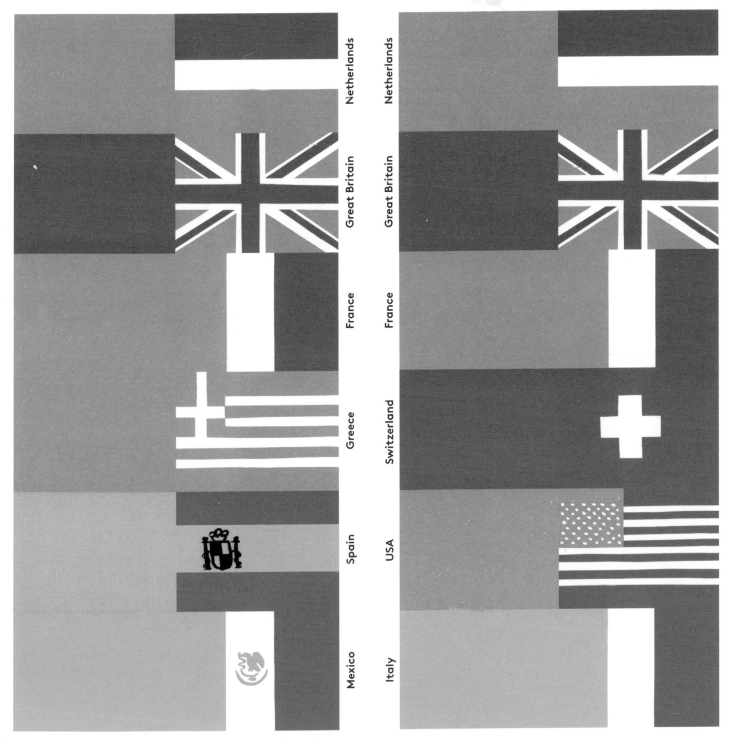

Netherlands

Netherlands

Great Britain

Great Britain

France

France

Greece

Switzerland

Spain

USA

Mexico

Italy

make your own cheese board flags!

labels for your homemade cheese

silly cheese stickers